Making Sanctuary Cities

I0120738

Anthropology of Policy

Cris Shore and Susan Wright, editors

Making Sanctuary Cities

Migration, Citizenship, and Urban Governance

Rachel Humphris

Stanford University Press
Stanford, California

Stanford University Press
Stanford, California

© 2025 by Rachel Humphris. All rights reserved.

No part of this book may be reproduced or transmitted in any form or by any means, electronic or mechanical, including photocopying and recording, or in any information storage or retrieval system, without the prior written permission of Stanford University Press.

Library of Congress Cataloging-in-Publication Data

Names: Humphris, Rachel, author.
Title: Making sanctuary cities : migration, citizenship, and urban
    governance / Rachel Humphris.
Other titles: Anthropology of policy (Stanford, Calif.)
Description: Stanford, California : Stanford University Press, 2025. |
    Series: Anthropology of policy | Includes bibliographical references and index.
Identifiers: LCCN 2024042788 (print) | LCCN 2024042789 (ebook) | ISBN
    9781503642218 (cloth) | ISBN 9781503642393 (paperback) | ISBN
    9781503642386 (ebook)
Subjects: LCSH: Sanctuary cities—Case studies. | Noncitizens—Government
    policy—Case studies. | Emigration and immigration—Government
    policy—Case studies. | Immigrants—Civil rights—Case studies. |
    Citizenship—Case studies. | Urban policy—Case studies.
Classification: LCC JV6271 (print) | LCC JV6271 (ebook) | DDC
    323.6/31—dc23/eng/20250107
LC record available at https://lccn.loc.gov/2024042788
LC ebook record available at https://lccn.loc.gov/2024042789

Cover design: Daniel Benneworth-Gray
Cover art: Richard Branczik, *City View*, 2020; acrylic on paper, 170 cm × 140 cm; private collection, Hereford, England
Typeset by Newgen in 10.5/15 Brill

Contents

Acknowledgments

There are so many people who gave their energy, support, and enthusiasm for this project. Ethnographic books rely on a lot of people to give up a lot of time. Those who spoke to me were already overburdened with multiple demands that were far more pressing than talking to a researcher. I encountered such kindness and generosity throughout the research process. In particular, Angela Romano who had such an inspiring approach to supporting young people in San Francisco. It really helped me to reflect on my role as a teacher and a citizen in the world. I will always be indebted to Angela Chan, who made me feel so welcome while explaining in painstaking detail the history of the sanctuary city in San Francisco. You taught me how to organise within and outside systems and how to really question power and its effects. You are truly an inspiration. Annette Wong taught me what it felt like to be included and welcomed in spaces that felt very new and was so patient when I asked very basic questions. Angela Greenwood gave up a lot of time explaining and helping me navigate local government procedures and processes in Sheffield. My heartfelt thanks to Mike Fitter for his ongoing curiosity, open-mindedness, and support of this project. It is very rare to find someone so committed and so open to learn. I hope that I have learned this from you. Also, to Stuart Barton who was always a friendly ear away from home. Thank you also to John Grayson—if only more people were like you, I don't think we would have the migration system we have today in the UK.

I am very grateful to Rabia Din for her time, energy, and interest in this project and my huge thanks to Macdonald Scott. Your tireless work is truly inspirational. Thank you also to Rebecca Cheff and Nadjla Banei for taking so much time to explain the intricacies of the healthcare system and inviting me to so many fascinating meetings and trainings. You have taught me how to be creative and keep going even when it seems like the odds are stacked against you. I'm also so grateful to the Southern Ontario Sanctuary Group, and everyone who welcomed me with such kindness and generosity throughout the winter of 2019. I always looked forward to Tuesday mornings despite the cold.

This research project was funded by the Leverhulme Trust Early Career Fellowship. The funding began when I was a post-doctoral researcher at IRiS, University of Birmingham. It wouldn't have got off the ground without the twin forces of Jenny Phillimore and Nando Sigona. You have both given me so much. I am also so grateful to my new home at Queen Mary University of London (QMUL) who warmly welcomed an anthropologist into their politics and international relations community. In particular, Engin Isin, who created such a unique atmosphere of critical and generous conversations in the Mobile People Programme. I feel so lucky to have joined QMUL because of these and so grateful that these conversations continue. I am also extremely grateful to Cris Shore and Susan Wright for their unparalleled editorial support.

I also found institutional homes in each city where I conducted fieldwork. Thank you to Jennifer Hyndman, Michaela Hynie, and all those at the Centre for Refugee Studies at York University. Thank you, Trisha Wood for all those delicious lunches—I truly enjoyed all our conversations. Thank you to Irene Bloemraad and everyone at the Sociology Department at UC Berkeley. The conversations as part of the Berkeley Interdisciplinary Migration Initiative really helped form a lot of the arguments in this book. In particular, I am hugely grateful to Cybelle Fox, for such inspiring conversations accompanied by the best wine. Thank you to Michele Lancione for the warm welcome to Sheffield and everyone at the City Centre.

There are also so many colleagues who I consider dear friends: Francesca Meloni, thank you for always being there in these changing times. Tanya Aberman, thank you for helping me feel like Toronto could be home even if just for three months. I am always in awe of your amazing work. Graham Hudson, thank you for helping me get through lockdown. Kathy Coll, thank you for all the encouragement, for helping me find my voice and the best hugs.

This book has taken many years, and it doesn't feel real that some of those who are part of this book and were so generous and kind are no longer with us. Gina Clayton was such an inspirational woman who achieved so much in Sheffield. Her energy and sharp thinking to advance the causes of migrants is so sadly missed. Francisco Rico-Martinez, who welcomed me to Toronto with a glass of wine and invited me to make empanadas in the kitchen with Loly, his wife, was a true inspiration. I learned so much even from the short amount of time that I spent at FCJ Refugee Centre. I also feel honoured to have known Michael Creal who provided such thoughtful comments on this research project and kindly shared his deep knowledge of refugee organising in Toronto. His work lives on through so many in Toronto and beyond.

I started writing this book in the Covid pandemic. It goes without saying that the support and love of my family got me through that extremely isolating and difficult time that was so full of loss. And it simply would not have been possible without Will. Writing this book has marked one of the biggest changes in our life with the arrival of our daughter. This book is dedicated to her.

INTRODUCTION
Why Sanctuary?

Sanctuary is really about: who belongs here? Who gets to decide? And why?

Laura, migrant activist, San Francisco

It is 9 January 2019, ten days before I meet Laura, and I have just arrived in San Francisco from London. I have not yet spotted the first of many Donald Trump piñatas or eaten the fresh corn tortillas that would become one of my favourite foods here. On the news, US Immigration and Customs Enforcement (ICE) are holding children in cages on the US border with Mexico. In a couple of weeks, I will attend a rally outside the Ninth Circuit Appeal Court where the US Constitution will be tested by sanctuary cities.[1] The stakes of the sanctuary city never seemed so clear in their potential as bastions of safety against rising anti-migrant hostility.

Throughout 2019, I lived in San Francisco (USA), Sheffield (UK), and Toronto (Canada) because they had all self-defined as 'sanctuary cities'. Sanctuary cities are often defined as cities that welcome or protect undocumented migrants from national immigration enforcement. These three cities were the first to specifically include this designation in their municipal government policies in each of their respective countries.[2] I wanted to understand why these cities had originated the term. Were there any common factors that could explain why they had become among the first cities to establish this movement? Did they really make a difference on the ground? How? I was drawn to these questions because I had previously researched welfare service providers who made discretionary decisions about whether to allow migrants access to services (often deciding based on moral judgements of deservingness). Sanctuary cities seemed to be addressing exactly these kinds of issues.[3] I spent three months in each city volunteering in migrants' rights organisations and interviewing people who were working with sanctuary city policy. I was immediately surprised by peoples' conflicting ideas about sanctuary cities, their effects, and what they should or could be.

One of these people was Laura, the child of undocumented Nicaraguan parents. Now a mother herself, living, working, and bringing up her young daughter in the Mission District, a predominantly Latinx neighbourhood of San Francisco, Laura had been organising for migrants' rights since she was a teenager. Her understanding of the sanctuary city, and what it could mean, stemmed from her everyday experiences living and organising alongside her family and neighbours who held many different legal migration statuses (and none). I met her by accident as I was interviewing Lena, the volunteer coordinator of a faith-based organisation in the basement of a church in the south of the Mission District. She rushed into the church on her way to a small office located at the back of the basement. Lena introduced me and Laura decided to join our conversation, sitting around a large wooden table. We discussed the sanctuary city for almost two hours before she had to rush to pick up her daughter from day care. She lucidly explained the enormous challenges to the sanctuary city but was limitless in her optimism and hope about what it could achieve. She bemoaned how sanctuary organising had lost its way because 'we have become service providers. We aren't a movement anymore.' But she hadn't dropped the term and continued to organise under the umbrella of the sanctuary city. I found myself not only inspired but also deeply moved by her stories, commitment, and aspirations.

Many others like Laura gave up large amounts of their time to explain to me in painstaking detail about their work and how they were continuing their struggles in the face of hugely difficult circumstances (which were about to get a lot harder with the outbreak of global pandemic in early 2020). However, the more people I spoke to, the more variations in the notion of sanctuary cities emerged. Some activists claimed the sanctuary city was useless and even worsened the situation. Others vowed that the sanctuary city was the most important part of their work and helped them achieve a wide range of different social justice struggles, from language classes to fighting evictions and deportations. For some the sanctuary city was used by the right-wing press to represent progressive immigrant policies in cities and fuel anti-migrant fears. Others claimed the sanctuary city was key to their decolonial agenda and fight for indigenous rights (for example the Toronto-based 'No

One Is Illegal on Stolen Land' campaign). Some activists disavowed the term all together, stating 'that's the term they use', referring to the municipal government, while others were setting up organisations foregrounding sanctuary. I found these contradictions not only in my fieldwork but also in the academic literature and policy debate about sanctuary cities.

These wide-ranging meanings and practices of the sanctuary city made researching them daunting. I was also unsure what could be gained from comparing sanctuary city policies across these three cities while retaining these different perspectives. I came to realise that this was not a problem, but the beginning of an answer. Inspired by my previous anthropological research, I thought about how I could, in the words of Susan Wright and Sue Reinhold, 'study through' the sanctuary city (2011).[4] This approach not only called for a wide variety of methods but also raised different kinds of questions. I call this approach 'comparative policy ethnography' (see Appendix 1). It ensures that one narrative doesn't dominate over others but foregrounds different people's evolving and potentially contradictory perspectives.

Crucially, comparative policy ethnography allowed me to attend to how the sanctuary city played out in situated contexts. The sanctuary city was always constituted for specific reasons, and at particular moments in time, and this made it difficult to pin down. It was not a fixed status to define nor a linear process to map. It was made up of practices that required elaboration and exploration in context.

This approach led me to question why and how, across such different contexts and intense contestation in each city, the sanctuary city was so salient? Why and how, amid such contradictions and confusions, was that term still being used with such passion? Why did sanctuary cities cause these tensions? And what was really at stake in claiming to be a sanctuary city?

This book sets out to answer these questions. I describe how the sanctuary city has emerged in each of these three cities, why, and with what effects. It is only then we can understand what 'work' the sanctuary city is doing. The quote from Laura that opened this chapter articulates why this matters. Sanctuary cities speak to the foundational basis on which we form, in Bridget Anderson's words, a 'community of value' (2013). Sanctuary cities provoke reflection on the kind of communities we want to create and the grounds on which we determine membership and belonging to those communities. The tensions sanctuary cities evoke reveal the contradictions in the values we value and, in so doing, open broader questions about how we live, organise our relations to others, and who we want to become. One reason sanctuary cities hold such 'weight' (Dave, Co-director of Sheffield migrant organisation) or 'energy' (Nicole, San Francisco District Attorney's office) is precisely because they evoke these enduring and fundamental questions.

Introducing Sanctuary in San Francisco, Sheffield, and Toronto

I introduce each city in the chronological order they declared themselves to be a sanctuary city (which was also the order of my fieldwork visits). Turning to San Francisco first, it is important to note that the USA is a country of migration through settler colonialism, and it has a restrictive migration policy and no overarching integration or settlement policy. San Francisco is in California, a pro-immigrant US state, passing a 'Sanctuary State' law (SB 54) in 2017 which forbids state and local officers from cooperating with federal immigration authorities in certain circumstances. California is also extremely wealthy. In 2022, if California were a country, it would be the fifth largest economy in the world.[5] San Francisco also has a strong and growing economy and is largely progressive. The city has a reputation for being one of the most liberal in the United States. It holds a dominant position in popular imagination as the home of Haight-Ashbury hippies and gay rights, immortalised in the memorials to Harvey Milk, the first openly gay elected politician in California.

The first thing that struck me about San Francisco when I lived there between January and April 2019, was inequality. Homelessness and poverty were painfully evident. Inequality was also placed into stark relief by odd facts that I was told about the city such as there are more dogs than children in San Francisco. Low-income families have been evicted and higher-income families believe San Francisco is too dangerous to bring up children. The city has become the home of 'Tech Giants', global technology companies which dominated the downtown area (Brahinsky 2014; Hartman 2002; McElroy 2019). While this has meant that the city could raise considerable funds from its tax base (Storper et al. 2016) and therefore could offer precaritised residents[6] access to city-funded welfare services, the growth of the technology industry has been responsible for widespread gentrification, pushing those that would benefit from these policies from the city.[7] Maharawal argues that the new tech-boom is distinguished in its 'total saturation of the city's rental and real estate markets' and has precipitated an 'eviction epidemic' (2017, 341).[8]

The city currently has the highest levels of income inequality (ibid.) and the most expensive rental market in the country.[9] These dynamics dramatically shape the sanctuary city as eviction of precaritised residents blurs the boundary between internal displacement and international deportations due to the concomitant loss of services. Evicted residents are predominantly Latinx or from the Asian Pacific Islander (API) population. African Americans are also the most rapidly declining group in San Francisco due to gentrification and eviction. These residents often have family and have been living in the city for decades (Mirabal 2009; Opillard 2015; Solnit 2000). The overriding feeling I got from San Francisco was that the city was changing too quickly, and it was a victim of its own success.

I was also struck by how many sanctuary actors[10] talked about their own situated positionality and 'taking stock of their privilege'. More so than the other two cities, sanctuary actors were engaged with academic writing, mentioning Els De Graauw's excellent book about sanctuary to me (2016). The city had a highly developed non-profit sector funded by city government and private philanthropy. San Francisco is a diverse city with 34 per cent foreign born residents[11] and many long-standing racialised groups such as Chinese migrants who began arriving in the city in the 1840s. In 2019, an estimated 6 per cent of residents (49,000) had no legal migration status.[12]

San Francisco designated itself as a sanctuary city in 1985. My interlocutors narrated three important stages in the development of the sanctuary city (for details see Mancina 2016 and Humphris 2021). First, the creation of the City of Refuge Ordinance in 1985 and strengthened in 1989. Crucially, much of this sanctuary organising stemmed from US military intervention in Central America. The tireless work of migrant rights activists reframed sanctuary as a city-level issue through building solidarity between Central American refugees and Mexican migrant workers. Chapters 12H and 12I of the Administrative Code imposed restrictions on all City and County of San Francisco employees not to ask, and obligations not to report, migration status to the federal government. Within two months all government applications, questionnaires, and interview forms used in relation to benefits, services or opportunities had been reviewed and all questions regarding immigration status were deleted.

The next significant moment for the sanctuary city in San Francisco came in 2008. In the wake of the 2006 Sensenbrenner Bill, a network of lawyers, advocates, and service providers, funded by the municipal government, organised against the deportation of undocumented youth. They launched the 'Due Process for Youth' Ordinance, which prohibited city officials from alerting federal immigration authorities when a person under eighteen was arrested on felony charges and did not have a legal migration status. Following on from the success of this policy, the 'Due Process for All' Ordinance was passed in 2013 as a response to the federal government's 'Secure Communities' programme. The programme asked that authorities hold undocumented residents charged with any crime in custody, even if they would normally be released, so federal agents could consider deportation. Under the new ordinance, unless an individual had a prior serious conviction, San Francisco officials would be unable to keep the person in custody based solely on immigration status.

The third significant stage began when commitments to the sanctuary city deepened after the election of Donald Trump. He tried to block federal grants to the city unless it cooperated with federal immigration officers, pushing the US Constitution to its limits. San Francisco's response included multiple municipal departmental memos to ensure adherence to sanctuary ordinances, city-level funding for a new Public Defender Immigration Unit to represent residents facing deportation, and a reinvigorated 'Rapid Response Network' to notify attorneys of ICE raids, among many other community responses detailed later in this book.

Moving to the UK's first sanctuary city, Sheffield is in Yorkshire, a region in the post-industrial north of the country. In 2021, it was the fifth largest city in the UK, with 14 per cent foreign born and 19 per cent black or 'other minority ethnic heritage'.[13] Sheffield City Council (SCC) is historically progressive. The County Council provoked the nickname 'Socialist Republic of South Yorkshire'. The majority of Sheffield's residents identified with Labour and it did not take long for people in the city to voice their strongly held views against the national Conservative Government in power at the time. Sanctuary actors also proudly talked about their Muslim mayor, a Somali refugee who grew up in the infamous Burngreave area of Sheffield. Despite sanctuary actors' left-wing proclivities and the widespread and long-standing commitment to the Labour party, there was an increasing far-right presence in the city (Grayson 2014). Similarly to San Francisco, I was shocked by the inequality in Sheffield. I was told about the film *Fairness on the 83* which charts a drop in healthy life expectancy of 20 years along the 83-bus route from one end of Sheffield to the other (Millhouses to Ecclesfield).

These inequalities had been exacerbated by the severe budget cuts that Sheffield, like all local authorities in the UK, experienced since the 2010 national government policy of austerity. Over the last decade, the funding from national government reduced by 30 per cent or £856 less per resident in real terms (Sheffield City Council 2023). Sheffield had a high density of non-profit organisations who have worked tirelessly to fill in the gaps left by shrinking public services. When I lived there between May and August 2019, I was surprised by the amount of volunteering and charity donations in the city that seemed to keep many organisations afloat. However, while some areas sunk into deprivation, central areas were being regenerated and there was a large amount of construction work. The advertising around these construction sites depicted high-end private student apartments with a concierge, gym, swimming pool, and cinema. These apartments appealed to wealthy international students attending the two large universities in the city.

While Sheffield may not be considered a 'global city' on the same terms as San Francisco or Toronto, it was shaped by similar trends of real-estate speculation, gentrification, and the deepening of long-standing inequalities (Rousseau 2009; Madanipour 2018). Regeneration projects began in Sheffield from the 1980s following the Thatcher government's destruction of the steel industry after the 1980s steel workers' strike. Scholars argue SCC coordinated speculative real-estate investment without durable connections to the local economy or taking account of the city's social capacities and needs (Clavel and Kraushaar 1998). Economic downturns revealed the limitations in these forms of urban governance as social inequalities widened. It has been argued that the Labour Government was adept at incorporating and containing radical challenges (Diamond 2021). Its long rule in Sheffield illustrates its success at absorbing these challenges.

Under a national and city-level Labour Government, Sheffield became the first city in the UK to adopt the term 'sanctuary city'. The Sheffield City of Sanctuary declaration was a commitment by the city to welcome people in need of safety and was agreed by SCC (SCC) in June 2007. In contrast to San Francisco, there has been no formal policy or statement by SCC or the City Mayor on the issue since the original declaration. Significantly, 'City of sanctuary' was not only a self-designation made by the city but also the name given to a charitable non-profit organisation called City of Sanctuary Sheffield (CoSS). More widely across the UK, City of Sanctuary also became a national grassroots movement (Allen 2020). CoSS signed up to the national City of Sanctuary Birmingham Declaration in 2014. The Birmingham Declaration was drawn upon in recent discussions with SCC regarding what sanctuary means in Sheffield (City of Sanctuary 2014). It provides five principles: all asylum seekers, refugees and migrants should be treated with dignity and respect; there should be a fair and effective process to decide whether people need protection; indefinite detention should end; destitution should end; and all migrants should be integrated, including free language class provision. The Birmingham Declaration places no duties on city governments to act on these principles.

This lack of commitment is not surprising given UK municipalities' limited power to diverge from national government policy. Unlike Canada and the USA, the UK is a unitary, not federal national government. In addition, since 2012, cities of sanctuary in the UK faced increasing pressure because the UK Government introduced a policy of creating a 'hostile environment' for migrants. The UK Government has systematically created internal migration checks termed by scholars as 'everyday bordering' (Yuval Davis et al. 2019).

The majority of precaritised residents in Sheffield live in a downscaled area of the city called Burngreave. According to the 2021 census, 30 per cent of Burngreave's residents self-identified as Asian, 16 per cent Black, and 8 per cent Arab.[14] This area, which was already subject to saturated policing, was the target of new private housing officers who were to cooperate with the Home Office, sparking the 'sanctuary moment' detailed in Chapter 5. It is extremely difficult to gauge the demographic profile of precaritised residents in Sheffield. Recent estimates suggest there are between 800,000 and 1.2 million people with no legal migration status in the UK. The most significant region of origin for the UK's undocumented population is Asia (52 per cent) followed by sub-Saharan Africa (20 per cent), the Americas and non-EU

Europe (16 per cent), and the Middle East/North Africa (11 per cent). The UK's undocumented communities are thought to be more settled than those in Europe, with over half having lived here for more than five years. Just over a quarter of undocumented people (215,000) are children, half of whom were born in the UK (Joint Council for the Welfare of Immigrants 2024). Similarly to San Francisco, it is likely that the undocumented population in Sheffield is increasingly long-standing with families and established lives in the city.

Finally to Toronto, which has a reputation for being one of the most diverse cities in the world. Canada is a country of migration through settler colonialism with a developed settlement strategy that is purportedly positive towards migrants, although scholars argue it is welcoming only to highly skilled migrants (Atak 2019). Since 2001, immigration to Toronto has been on the rise. In 2021, 47 per cent of the Greater Toronto Area (GTA) were immigrants.[15] More than half the city's population (56 per cent) identified as belonging to a 'racialised group' (City of Toronto 2022). Toronto City Government embraces this identity as a home for people from all over the world. The city hosts a dizzying array of different festivals and celebrations to mark the different backgrounds of its residents. I lived in Toronto between September and December 2019 and there were festivals outside City Hall almost every weekend. Restaurants also attest to this diversity, such as 'Rasta Pasta', one of my favourite places to eat in the bohemian Kensington Market area. I was also struck by the land acknowledgements that were read aloud before any official event. While these have been criticised as solely symbolic and a far-cry from providing reparations to Canada's indigenous population, they were notable because this never happened in San Francisco.

Canada has had only one Conservative premier, Stephen Harper, who served from 2004 to 2015. However, Toronto is situated in the state of Ontario which has been largely Conservative, with the Liberals forming a government for only five years out of sixty between 1943 and 2003. At the time of fieldwork, the Ontario premier, Doug Ford, was Conservative and staunchly anti-immigrant. Many sanctuary actors compared Doug Ford to Donald Trump, an association aided by their similar physical appearance. After hearing these comments, I noticed a large amount of anti-Ford graffiti in the city.

Toronto is a growing metropolis with a large amount of construction and 'urban revitalisation'. I attended a community event in the controversial

Regent's Park social housing development in a pristine community centre surrounded by new high-rise apartment buildings. While care had been taken to ensure 'right to return' for those evicted, the previous residents I met believed the project had failed them in various ways (James 2010). I was also surprised by the huge amount of building work on the waterfront. Sparkling high-rise apartment blocks stood imposingly on Lake Ontario's edge. Their private manicured gardens led directly to newly privatised parts of the waterfront, pushing pedestrians onto the highway.

My interlocutors narrated that organising for what became the sanctuary city in Toronto began in earnest in 2006 when the grassroots movement No One Is Illegal, Toronto (NOII), called for welfare services to adopt a 'Don't Ask, Don't Tell' policy. After several aggressive raids by the federal immigration authority, Canada Border Services Agency (CBSA), multiple campaigns emerged including 'Education not Deportation' (schools), 'Shelters, Sanctuary, Status' (shelters), Ontario Health Insurance Plan (OHIP) for all (healthcare), Food for all (food banks), and the 'Don't ask, don't tell' coalition (police).

These campaigns provided the groundwork for the 'Access T.O.' policy that was passed by the City Council in February 2013. At that time, estimates of the number of undocumented residents in the GTA ranged from 200,000 to 500,000 (Gastaldo et al. 2012). Access T.O. was termed a sanctuary city policy in the media and later, in January 2017 the then Mayor, John Tory, self-designated Toronto as a sanctuary city (Fox 2017). The Access T.O. policy obliges the city to ensure all Torontonians have access to the municipal services for which they are eligible 'without fear of reprisal with respect to status'. In practice, this means all municipal services should not make access dependent on providing legal migration status documents. These services are limited to emergency services, emergency shelter and housing support, by-law enforcement, employment help, library services, public health services, recreation programmes, garbage collection, and parks. Only library services and public health explicitly reference Access T.O. in their strategic policy. Other services that would make a material difference to Torontonians would require changes to provincial legislation (including the Education Act, the Ontario Works Act and Ontario Disability Act, the Ontario Police Services Act, and the Social Housing Act[16]).

Toronto can enact sanctuary city policies in practice through negotiations with federal and provincial governments. Canadian municipalities are generally considered to be 'creatures of provinces' but two factors allowed Toronto more room for manoeuvre. First, Metropolitan Toronto was amalgamated with its six lower-tier municipalities into a single City of Toronto in 1998, increasing its tax base. Second, Toronto has taken the lion's share of responsibility for Canada's settlement policy. Consequently, it has been afforded latitude in some areas of immigration governance (see Chapter 3). While Toronto has limited powers to raise its own budgets and therefore cannot offer the same level of funded welfare provision as San Francisco, federalism does provide the city with more leeway.

However, similarly to the other two cities, Toronto has undergone increasing gentrification and widening social inequalities. Toronto is a city in which the 'inner suburbs' became poorer and residents were racialised as 'ethnic minorities' while the professional classes were racialised as white and got richer. Post-amalgamation Toronto has become a highly differentiated space in which many areas are privileged while others suffer growing poverty and marginalisation, compounded by visible systemic racism.

Sanctuary in Racialised, Globalised, and Securitised Cities

The overriding commonality between these three sanctuary cities, despite their widely divergent histories, was that the targets of sanctuary city policies were predominantly visibly racialised low-income residents.[17] Moreover, these residents were concentrated in specific areas in each city.[18] These areas were subject to the same forms of community surveillance, pre-emptive stop-and-frisk policies, public order containment, saturated policing, and highly contingent access to services.[19] These policies and practices rely on logics of disposability and fungibility where 'the distinction that renders some deserving and others not is racialised so as to classify collectives in order to judge individuals' (Shilliam 2018, 171). In the area of migration, as scholars such as Bhagat (2022, 9–10) and Cross (2020, 72) have noted, these classifications operate through the dichotomies of 'legal' and 'illegal' migrant, 'authentic' and 'bogus' asylum seekers. One of the main aims of this book is to draw out the long-standing links between the racialised urban poor and those without a legal migration status and reveal the implications for sanctuary cities. As the book goes on to show, these links reveal the limits of sanctuary cities as well as their role in creating the conditions to contain some, for example in exploitative labour, while others are expelled (through forced rehousing, eviction or deportation).

I also noticed that precaritised residents did the same kinds of jobs in all three cities. They worked in dirty, dangerous, and devalued jobs such as construction or social care. Migration scholars have long argued that migrants do not just end up in these jobs due to a variety of factors that arise from 'somewhere else'. Rather, migration is an internal feature of how capitalism functions at the global scale. The movement of capital relentlessly generates movement of people, which, in turn, is constitutive of the concrete forms of capitalism itself. Moreover, scholars attribute intentionality to migrants' ascribed irregularity, which appears as a tool to perpetuate and codify their subordinate position within local and global labour markets (Mezzadra and Neilson 2013). Cities have been at the forefront of these developments, relying on cheap, precaritised migrant labour to make the city 'from below' (Sassen 2014).[20] A second aim of this book is to bring these insights into conversation with sanctuary cities to reveal how economic concerns and capital accumulation shape cities' responses to precaritised residents.

In addition, in all three countries, migrants are rendered 'useful' well beyond their capacity to be easily exploited in labour markets. Migrants have continuously figured in the so-called 'post-political' stalemate in North Atlantic societies, most starkly since the 11 September terrorist attacks in New York City, and in the aftermath of the 2008 financial crisis and its associated upheavals. The figure of the racialised migrant has become an overwhelming theme of populism as seen through the political campaigns of Donald Trump in the US, the Brexit debate in the UK, and Trudeau blaming immigrants for Canada's housing crisis. Migrants carry the blame for deepening social inequality. The idea of migration as a form of attack (signified in attempts to build defensive walls, close borders, stop 'small boats') has been normalised. Notions such as 'deservingness' and the 'good migrant' are dominating tropes across all three countries with little reckoning of how human mobility, race, and empire have been part of the exclusionary logic of nation-building and city-making since their inception. The third aim of this book is to trace the underlying logics behind these tropes and why they are so compelling, and provide a historical reading of sanctuary cities that does not start with social movements in 1980s but is part of a longer history of governance shaping the relationship between population, territory, and wealth. The overall aim of the book is to trace sanctuary cities' competing moral values that construct pre-caritised residents as more or less deserving of rights and resources. I avoid defining sanctuary cities as either resistance to, or an extension of, restrictive national policies. Rather, I emphasise how the sanctuary city can be both.

The Book

The remainder of this book progresses across five chapters. Chapter 1 introduces the cities ethnographically through three events where the sanctuary city was 'made up', drawing out key theoretical and methodological concerns. The chapter details how sanctuary city discussions pivoted on considering who belonged and on what terms. It also demonstrates how the methodology of comparative policy ethnography provokes different questions that do not concern finding a definition of the sanctuary city. Rather this approach opens questions about how and why the idea of sanctuary is mobilised in the service of particular political projects and in order to solve common problems that emerge in all three cities.

Chapter 2 builds on current sanctuary city literature, to explore the historical ramifications of 'the city' and its (settler-) colonial dynamics. Through historical sociology and decolonial urban political economy it traces how the rise of modern statehood and market economies occurred at the same time as the subordination of the city to the nation as the only sovereign political community. The rise of modern states, and the making of colonialism on which capitalism relied, extended pre-modern urban concerns about sanitation, plague, crime, and disorder to colonial urban governance (Goldberg 2002; Shilliam 2018). The responsibilities of modern city government became the key instrument for disciplining the poor, accompanied by moral justifications that still hold weight today. The chapter links these developments within the shared colonial history of the book's Anglosphere three-country comparison as a shared space of law and governance.

The insights revealed in Chapter 2 help to reformulate a recurring question about sanctuary cities, explored in Chapter 3. We should not ask whether cities can act autonomously but rather what specific kinds of governing rights and obligations cities possess, for what purposes, and who is invested with these powers. The chapter places the three cities within their legal constitutions, as municipalities within three differently structured nation-states. This chapter provides the political, social, and economic contexts that shape the moral values about precaritised residents.

Chapter 4 lays out the mutable and contingent moral values that emerge in the practice of the sanctuary city that I categorise as: 'the efficient city', 'the safe city', and the 'just city'. The chapter explores how these moral conceptions are constantly in motion and accounts for how 'progressive' moral orientations can end up supporting and sustaining neoliberal systems. Chapter 5 explores how these moralities are translated into practices. The chapter includes ethnographic policy analysis of a defining sanctuary moment in each city. These moments are conceived as instances when deference to dominant or official narratives that work to reinstate policy ambitions and conceal divergent and contradictory logics are disrupted. We can find meaning in these moments of tension, when there is friction, where governing systems momentarily seize up and new practices must emerge.

Overall, sanctuary cities are a strategic space where the city emerges as a 'battleground through which groups defined their identities, staked their claims, waged their battles and articulated citizenship rights, obligations and principles' (Isin 2002, 51). Questions of liberal citizenship are therefore at the heart of struggles over sanctuary cities.[21] Grassroots organisers like Laura, who opened this book, rejected notions of competition, commodification, and capital accumulation. They were working with moral values that were guided by a different relationship between people, place, and resources that were localised and personalised. Laura could be said to have 'rescaled' citizenship from national to urban or, in her words, 'belonging to community'. This rescaling challenges one of the essential projects of nation-building which has been to dismantle the historic primacy of urban citizenship and to displace it with the national, although it never managed to replace it entirely (Prak 2018). Crucially, this rescaling held most weight in a federalised nation-state indicating the importance of intermediary institutions such as states and provinces in restoring the urban as a site of affiliation and identification, against the nation.

The book elaborates how radical possibilities for achieving the promise of liberal citizenship (we are all equal) are translated into palatable policies for local government which, as we see in Chapter 5, can further institute inequalities.[22] This analysis reveals how liberal citizenship is undermined by the very thing that makes it worth investing in—the promise of equality. An ethnographically informed reading of sanctuary cities is crucial to tease out the potential of liberal citizenship but also the complex processes through which governing systems suffocate but never extinguish practices animated by radical potential.

To understand these processes, we must understand the moral values that underpin them. Focusing on moral values helps to explain why the notion of the sanctuary city resonates in the contemporary moment across such different people and places but also why it has not realised its promise of transformation. As the book shows, increasingly restrictive 'international' migration controls and 'domestic' border enforcement unsettled the fragile balance that had been in place between city and nation, which had allowed cities to manage, to some extent, their own legitimacy of governing. Sanctuary cities provided a short-term, partial answer to these intractable dilemmas for urban policy makers that were always already constrained by their histories and embedded contexts. However, this is not a story of foreclosed politics. Rather the tensions that sanctuary cities evoke, the actions they trigger, and alternative ways of thinking about belonging, they inspire, hold openings and possibilities. Whether the 'sanctuary city' is the name given to these struggles in the future remains to be seen.

ONE
Performing Sanctuary
Making Sanctuary Cities Real

These are the people who clean our toilets, take care of our kids, do some of the most unwanted jobs, like in the construction industry, which is booming right now. There are huge numbers of people working here. Everybody knows it. What good is it to us, as a city, to marginalize, and make invisible and push these people underground? They're going to have higher disease rates, higher crime rates, because people are going to do what they need to do to eat and to live. And have all kinds of abuse of them. And rich countries know that bottom line. You want to deal with those folks in a coherent, consistent, holistic manner? And take them out? Your economy falls apart.

Nick, ex-councillor, Toronto City Government

This chapter introduces the cities ethnographically through moments of puzzlement where the sanctuary city is 'made up'. These three moments indicate the differences between the cities and how comparative policy ethnography can reveal the common underlying problems each city tried to solve through their own iterations of the 'sanctuary city'. The quote from Nick above gives an indication of these problems, namely that cities need precaritised migrant workers while nation-states scapegoat them and make them deportable. As will be shown in the next chapter, these problems are related to the fundamental tensions in governing that stemmed from the relationship between population, territory and wealth in North Atlantic societies.

Before moving to that historical context, this chapter provides detail about how I came to produce ethnography in each city, how I made relationships, my motivations and points of entry.[1] Comparative policy ethnography addresses how and why the sanctuary city is mobilised in the service of particular political projects. Rather than solely focusing on the detailed content of sanctuary practices this methodology places emphasis on the relations and processes that give rise to and shape them. This approach reveals the common tensions in each city that sanctuary city policies had tried to resolve.[2]

This methodological approach resonates with Gillian Hart's view of 'relational comparison' (2018). She defines three nodes to think about the methodology and theory of relational comparison. First, she argues it is important to define the 'relational' in relational comparison as dialectical (but not teleological nor totalising). Second, she rejects the notion of pre-given 'cases' to focus on spatio-historical specificities as well as interconnections and mutually constitutive processes. This point dovetails with Linda Peake's call to think about different sites not as distinct cases but as 'windows into embedded practices' (Peake 2019). Third, Hart urges us to think conjuncturally, bringing key forces at play in each city into the same frame of analysis as connected yet distinctively different nodes in globally interconnected historical geographies. Thinking with Hart, I present the three cities through an ethnographic vignette in the order in which they declared themselves to be sanctuary cities (San Francisco, Sheffield, and Toronto) which was also the order in which I conducted my fieldwork visits.

San Francisco

It's 11 February 2019 and I've now been living in San Francisco for just more than a month. I have conducted thirty-six interviews with various sanctuary actors including directors of municipal services, legislative aides to Supervisors (elected members of the municipal government), doctors, lawyers, nonprofit workers, community support officers, and volunteers (see Appendix 1). I chose these interviewees through an open-ended and flexible approach due to the variety of places in and through which sanctuary cities emerged and to remain oriented towards the relational, fleeting, and mobile. I started in the same way for each city. While reading relevant academic and grey literature I made notes of all organisations that had written reports or were mentioned as playing an important role in the making of the sanctuary city. When reviewing policy documents, I noted who submitted comments, opinions, and petitions, deputed at committee hearings or were listed as members of relevant working groups or committees. I also searched for relevant organisations through strategic reports or networks in each city. I contacted all these organisations, or if the organisation had closed, I traced those mentioned to their new positions to ask for an interview. These interviews then expanded into attending training sessions or meetings such as the ones I describe below as well as volunteering in migrant rights' organisations and attending any other relevant community or policy event.

It was quarter to six in the evening, and I was walking through Chinatown towards the Chinatown YMCA. I had already conducted two interviews that day. The first with the Director of the Public Defender's Immigration Unit, a service set up to provide public defenders in the wake of Donald Trump's threats of mass deportations of undocumented San Franciscans. The second with the Director of San Francisco's Adult Probation Department. This department had previously communicated with ICE to inform them when an undocumented resident was being released from custody; however, they had recently changed this policy. My head was swimming with thoughts from these very different interviews. I also tried to switch from my role as an interviewer of professional bureaucrats to participant observer entering a community space in the evening (I had also changed my clothes from a suit to jeans). I had done this kind of switching throughout my fieldwork so far and would continue to do so throughout the next year of producing data.[3]

I had visited this YMCA twice before. I had contacted Anyu, the YMCA CEO, because the organisation was part of the US 'Welcoming City' movement, which had a policy exchange programme with UK City of Sanctuary. I emailed Anyu who agreed to an interview but stated the Welcoming City initiative had not been relevant to them because those who used the YMCA had been living in the city for generations. To help me understand their work she introduced me to two of her support workers, Peter and Mia. They invited me to this community information session about the sanctuary city. The session was being run by a Chinese advocacy group who I already knew because I had interviewed Diana, the policy director of the organisation. I had found her because she was listed as part of the team who organised for the 'Due Process for Youth' Ordinance in a report submitted to the San Francisco Board of Supervisors.

Despite knowing those running the session I was still a bit nervous. I entered the YMCA and was immediately struck by the familiar smell of chlorine from the swimming pool. People with gym bags were coming in and out. No one was at reception because it was six o'clock. I had no idea where the community session was being held and almost all the signs were in Chinese. I wandered around and finally found a staircase and decided to try upstairs. The smell of chlorine and children's happy swimming noises faded. I came across a large room with a PowerPoint presentation set up at one end. At the other was a long table with a row of large stainless steel catering trays full of different kinds of stews, rice, and vegetables. Eight round tables of between five and ten people filled the rest of the room. I stood by the door a bit perplexed. I recognised Diana, who was serving food. The majority of those being served were older people speaking Cantonese (I found out later). My feelings of being out of place mounted and I considered leaving having already had a long day. However, Peter, the support worker who invited me, spotted me loitering at the door and invited me in. Diana piled a plate full of food with a warning that it might be a bit spicy for me and I perched on a piano stool at the back of the room eating from my flimsy paper plate.

The session started as two people, a man and a woman, much younger than the majority of those sitting at the tables, stood up by the PowerPoint presentation and introduced themselves as Matteo and Mei-Ying. Peter pulled up a chair and came to sit next to me. He told me he couldn't translate because Matteo was speaking Cantonese, and he only spoke Mandarin. After a few minutes Diana came to stand behind me, leaning on the piano, and spent the next thirty minutes simultaneously translating the session. When Mei-Ying spoke, Peter took over the translation because it switched to Mandarin. I kept telling them how grateful I was for their hard work, and they smiled and carried on.

Matteo and Mei-Ying played a video from Chinese media about the evils of the sanctuary city. It depicted the case of Kate Steinle, a young blonde woman living in San Francisco who had been shot and killed in 2015 by a Latinx man who it emerged was undocumented. The case had been used by Donald Trump in his election campaign to fuel anti-migrant hostility. Diana told me this news programme was extremely popular and was heavily informed by right-wing politics, 'a bit like Fox news', she added.

Matteo went through the main points about the sanctuary city trying to 'myth-bust' the news programme. He focused on the fact that local police can't enforce federal government immigration laws. He reiterated that no one should ask about immigration status when accessing any services in the city and that anyone was safe to go to the police. Mei-Ying went through what sanctuary meant in California more broadly. She explained that the city had stronger laws than in California, but that San Francisco was helping those outside the city as well through campaigning for the Sanctuary State law (SB 54).

The session shifted as each table was instructed to look at the stories of two different people that were printed on hand-outs. The first was a woman from the Philippines who was sentenced to twenty-two years in prison and then was deported. An older gentleman sitting on the table in front of me said that she should have been deported straight away. Or she should have gone to jail and then stayed in the USA. His justification was based on the money she cost the taxpayer by being kept in prison. A younger lady at the same table, the mother of a young child who was sitting beside her, said that she should have been deported straight away. As Diana translated for me, she explained that the young woman had justified her decision stating, 'if you commit a crime you can't stay. Those are the rules'. An older lady on the other side of the room thought that the woman in the story must have done something very bad due to the length of her sentence and therefore should have been deported straight away. A younger lady noted in a quiet voice that it didn't matter because, as Diana translated, 'it's all racial discrimination'. Mei-Ying agreed with this participant and brought up the 1882 Chinese Exclusion Act and the history of Chinese people in San Francisco, explaining how deportations were a new iteration of the same process. However, very quickly an older woman participant said that history didn't matter. They should be thinking about now, particularly the young people today who have nowhere to live.

In my notes that I made after the event I wrote 'Mia' next my description of this interaction. Mia was a YMCA support worker, and had mentioned when I interviewed her how she had grown up in Chinatown but now had to live a two hour commute away. Chinatown was extremely overcrowded, and tech-induced gentrification had fragmented families because young tech professionals wanted to rent flats close to the downtown area. As mentioned in the Introduction, the transnational flow of ideas, goods, images, and persons intensified by recent developments in the urbanisation of capital has resulted in a new form of urbanism: a neoliberal mode of urban governance characterised by redevelopment, urban expansion, and real-estate speculation. Evictions in San Francisco were at an all-time high due to this reworking of the city. Peake and Rieker summarise these trends as, 'processes of disassemblage and reconstitution of the social—disintegration of family and community, the displacement of the poor, regulatory (and increasingly securitized) infrastructure, and violence' (2013, 14). Families in Chinatown were at the sharp end of these processes.

Returning to the YMCA, the discussion then turned to the second story which detailed a young Vietnamese boy who didn't pay his Muni fare (bus ticket). He got caught by the police and was deported because he was undocumented. There was general agreement in the room that he should have been deported because he didn't pay. Then someone noted that the story detailed he forgot his wallet at home that contained his Muni pass. Those who had been very vocal all laughed dispelling the uncomfortable moment when this relatable action was revealed. Peter and Mei-Ling asked open questions regarding what the residents' thought was fair, provoking them to think about the morality involved in deporting those who had been convicted of a crime and where to draw the line.

Throughout the discussion about the two stories no one mentioned the sanctuary city. It seemed as though the residents did not think the sanctuary city did anything for them. I spoke to Diana about this after the session. She was not surprised that many thought that the sanctuary city harbours criminals and that it doesn't affect them because they listen to ethnic Chinese media that repeats fearmongering about illegal immigrants and criminals. She explained this was why they continued to do these information sessions and had begun to shift the notion of the sanctuary city to include those who were being evicted as well as those deported to broaden support. Diana held memories of organising for the sanctuary city through the 'Due Process for Youth' Ordinance in 2009. She knew the Public Defender I had spoken to earlier in the day because they had organised together for that ordinance. She held this embodied memory as she explained that the sanctuary city had to keep changing because the boundaries kept changing. She also explained how she was encouraging the 'next generation' of organisers. She introduced me to Mei-Ying who I had seen at rallies I attended to support the sanctuary city. Mei-Ying explained to me that she was a directly affected resident and would be happy to share her experiences. She shared her email with me and agreed to meet for a coffee.

As I walked to the bus stop after the meeting, I reflected on how busy the streets were and how overcrowded this part of the city was. On the bus home I wrote up the notes from this session and the conflicting meanings of the sanctuary city that had played out. I emailed Mei-Ying to set up a time for us to have coffee and checked my diary for the interviews I was conducting tomorrow in the Mission District, the predominantly Latinx area of San Francisco which encountered many of the same issues but had a very different demographic profile. Overall, this community information event reveals how the sanctuary city was used to think about who belongs to the city and on what terms very explicitly. Activists in San Francisco were aware that the sanctuary city relied on building a community who considered precaritised residents as belonging on the same terms as others. For example, the sanctuary city relied on residents to alert the Rapid Response Network if they saw a neighbour being detained by ICE and to vote for local representatives who supported progressive migration policies. The challenges of this work were also very forcefully made clear particularly given the success of the right-wing media to scapegoat migrants and to make the sanctuary city seem irrelevant at best or dangerous and a waste of taxpayers' money at worst. Activists used notions of 'fairness' to provoke discussions about belonging and specifically to question some residents' certainty about the boundaries between 'deserving' and 'undeserving'. They were also expanding the meaning of the sanctuary city to include evictions as well as deportations.

Sheffield

It was almost two o'clock on 11 June 2019 and I was standing outside Sheffield Town Hall, a large, imposing stone building in the centre of the city that presides over the busy high street. I was attending my second 'Refugee and Migrant Forum'. The forum took place every month and lasted for two hours. I found out about the forums because I volunteered at the reception desk of the non-governmental organisation 'City of Sanctuary Sheffield' (CoSS) which ran a building called 'The Sanctuary' just around the corner from the Town Hall. Political geographer, Jonny Darling, has comprehensively explored the relational dynamics of City of Sanctuary Sheffield (2010; Squire and Darling 2013) and I had extensively read his work before I started volunteering at this organisation. The Sanctuary was open during the day providing a warm space for anyone to come in and sit on the sofas. There was a kitchen where tea and coffee were served (provided free to asylum seekers). A free lunch was also served to asylum seekers once a week. In the basement, activities such as a choir and youth group took place. Upstairs various agencies including the British Red Cross and South Yorkshire Refugee Law and Justice helped asylum seekers and refugees with their legal cases or settlement issues. I walked with members of those organisations to the Town Hall.

We arrived at the same room as last month and took seats around the large wooden table that filled the room. I recognised almost everyone at this meeting because I had been living, volunteering, and interviewing people in the city for more than a month. There was a small network of organisations who worked with asylum seekers and refugees and members of those organisations had been very helpful and introduced me to others in the network. I realised that many had known each other for years and relationships were long-standing.

Jane, the director of CoSS, chaired the meeting and began by asking everyone to introduce themselves and their organisations. Other refugee and advocacy organisations in the city were represented including the Refugee Council, SCC's community development officer, Shelter, a refugee youth worker, an ESOL (English for speakers of other languages) worker, a housing worker from ASSIST Sheffield, an advocacy group South Yorkshire Migration and Asylum Action Group (SYMAAG), and the Sheffield representative of a national organisation that campaigns to stop detention and deportation. Two members of the private housing association, Mears, were also attending because they had just taken over the contract to provide housing for asylum seekers from the widely disparaged G4S.

I introduced myself as a researcher and briefly explained the research project again because I had already interviewed most people at the meeting and didn't want to take up too much time. I asked meeting attendees to come and talk to me if they had any questions about the project. I mentioned that I had just come back from San Francisco and was going to Toronto after Sheffield. Michelle, the community development officer, thought I should get a T-shirt with the three cities printed on it and seemed delighted that Sheffield was being compared to these two large North American cities.

The meeting began with the issue of asylum housing and the Mears representatives underwent particularly detailed questioning from Steve, a member of the advocacy organisation, SYMAAG. Asylum seeker housing was predominantly concentrated in one 'downscaled' area of the city where there were already multiple challenges around service provision and intensified policing and surveillance (see Introduction). Steve encouraged Mears to diversify the location of asylum seeker housing. After about thirty-five minutes the meeting turned to the next agenda item entitled 'Sheffield Council'. Michelle explained that the Home Office had approached Sheffield Council to pilot a new approach called 'Immigration Navigators'. They wanted to base national government officers in community venues such as 'The Sanctuary'. The aim, according to the Home Office, was to 'identify vulnerabilities', 'make UK Visas and Immigration (UKVI) more accessible', 'reduce the number of people who didn't have recourse to public funds' (NRPF) and to 'lessen the burden in Local Authorities'.

Jane asked attendees for their views on this proposal and silence descended on the meeting. It surprised me that no one around the large meeting table was immediately forthcoming to share their views. Finally, after the silence became uncomfortable and Jane and Michelle had encouraged attendees to voice their opinions about this pilot scheme, Molly, from a national migrants' rights campaigning group, started the discussion. She explained that she thought it would be a bad idea because voluntary organisations would find it difficult to retain trust with the community if they hosted these 'Immigration Navigators'.

Basmah, a Red Cross support worker, explained that she had met with the Home Office and found out that the 'Immigration Navigators' would ask clients for ID. She explained that her organisation had decided against hosting these navigators because they would not be immigration experts and, therefore, they were not convinced that they could provide any additional support. Steve from SYMAAG joined in asking whether this was just a rebranding of ICE (Immigration Compliance and Enforcement) teams and invoked Sheffield as a City of Sanctuary. Through his intervention he infused the political back into discussions that had been rendered technical and bureaucratic. Jane agreed with Basmah that the Immigration Navigators would not bring additional support to organisations. As no organisations were interested, Michelle, as the representative from the Council at the meeting, noted that she would respond to the Home Office stating that they did not want to be involved in the pilot project.

The justification for the proposal that it would 'lessen the burden on Local Authorities' is noteworthy as it was emblematic of how central government had first reduced resources to local governments through austerity but then offered support through targeted programmes that fulfilled their own objectives. This process, known as 'austerity urbanism' indicates the down-loading, dismantling, and restriction of institutional supports for social repro-duction from the nation-state to local government (Peck 2012). Sheffield had extremely limited powers to raise funds from council tax and business rates. These funds were used to pay for statutory services with no additional funds to be able to support programmes for precaritised residents, increasing the pressure on Sheffield's municipal government.

It is also noteworthy that there was a long silence before any opinion was shared about the proposal. After the forum, I met Dave, co-director of a com-munity cohesion organisation, in a coffee shop. I brought up the silence at the Town Hall and that I was surprised it had taken so long for people to speak out against this proposal. We agreed that we thought everyone at the table would not have wanted to collaborate with the Home Office. Dave attributed the silence to 'British politeness'. I explained that I thought the silence indi-cated an uncertainty regarding others' views in the meeting. Dave agreed that there were potentially divergent opinions between organisations in the city and explained a tension that I heard throughout my time in Sheffield. There was a long-standing difference between organisations that believed in strict non-cooperation with national government and were openly 'polit-ical' and those that were funded to provide services and were purportedly non-political. In practice, the latter group often became entangled in govern-mental processes through their efforts to provide migrants' access to services. These different approaches towards the sanctuary city were more forcefully revealed in the 'sanctuary moment' detailed in Chapter 5.

Dave and I also discussed why Sheffield municipal government didn't more openly make statements about refusing to cooperate with these pilot programmes particularly when they were challenged by advocacy organ-isations for not doing enough to enact the sanctuary city. He explained municipal government's fear to mention the sanctuary city due to grow-ing right-wing sentiment that was particularly evident in the north of the city. The demonisation of migrants took many forms but particularly reso-nated with the notion that there were not enough resources to fund welfare services. This opinion proliferated even though precaritised residents did not receive welfare benefits but rather were working in exploitative con-ditions in construction, hand car washes, take away food outlets, and as care providers. Austerity urbanism and migrant scapegoating combined to silence the local government on the issue of the sanctuary city.

Toronto

On Friday 25 October 2019, I made my way to a meeting at the Workers' Action Center. I had been living in Toronto for two months and knew the walk down Bloor Street well from my apartment in Koreatown. It was a large, busy road that formed one of the main east to west grid roads of Toronto to the north of the downtown area. I passed my favourite Korean restaurant and the Asian supermarket where I did most of my grocery shopping. As the road became wider, the shop signs became less Korean, and I came to the intersection with Spadina Road. This road ran north to south through the heart of Toronto. This was my third visit to the Workers' Action Center, a large but quite unremarkable looking building. Previously, I had two of my most illuminating conversations in the café on the ground floor. Over coffee and pastries Owen and Nazir, two of the founding members of No One Is Illegal Toronto, detailed their memories of organising for precaritised residents in the city. I met Nazir at a trade union rally about gentrification in the city because he set up a migrant workers' organisation which was based in this building. I contacted Owen because he was the author of many reports and guides for service providers and precaritised residents providing advice about detention and deportation. He continued to be a lawyer giving legal advice and training to those who are working for the rights of precaritised residents in the city.

Rather than finding a seat in the café, I followed signs to the meeting and made my way upstairs to a training session organised by a group called Butterfly, the Asian and Migrant Sex Workers Support Network. It was an unusual Friday for me. I usually volunteered at the Roma Advice Center at the opposite end of Bloor Street where I practised Romani (a language learned during my doctoral studies) and learned about the challenges faced by precaritised Roma residents in Toronto. Today I was taking a week off to attend this training session. I came to know about the training because it was advertised through a group called the Rights of Non-Status Women Network (RNSWN). I had been attending the meetings of RNSWN since I arrived in Toronto because an academic told me about the group before I began my fieldwork.

Although I arrived on time the large room was already completely full of people arranged around circular tables. A small group of people were standing by a laptop at the front of the room preparing their presentations. I was immediately struck by the posters on the walls of the room depicting previous migrants' rights campaigns and perhaps, most strikingly, handprints adorned with the slogans 'hand jobs are jobs!' Some participants were taking selfies with these posters. I was drawn to do the same but was feeling a bit self-conscious and so went to the coffee room next door before returning to find a seat at one of the tables.

The training session ran for three hours. It was hosted by Butterfly's founder and director Hazel, an extremely persuasive and energetic speaker who welcomed everyone to the session and explained the challenges faced by migrant sex workers. She focused on how anti-trafficking regulations harmed migrant sex workers, particularly how the discourse of 'rescue' led to cooperation between by-law enforcement officers, police, and immigration enforcement. Hazel highlighted how this language of rescue has been used to depoliticise the deportation of migrant sex workers and how anti-trafficking legislation increased the surveillance of migrant sex workers in already highly policed areas. These laws contribute to the idea of 'raced space' where precaritised residents live in areas of the city that are subject to increased surveillance and intensive policing. She reviewed the Access T.O. policy and invoked Toronto's sanctuary city status. She explained that frontline workers, including by-law enforcement officers, should not ask about a resident's migration status and appealed to service providers' 'sense of justice'.

The training then became similar to the YMCA training in San Francisco. Each table was given the story of two people who had been deported because of cooperation between a by-law enforcement officer, the police, and immigration enforcement. In the first story, by-law enforcement officers inspected the massage parlour where 'Ding Ding' worked. They contacted the police because they thought she had been trafficked. The police asked her for her work permit which forbid her to work in the sex industry. The police reported her to Canada Border Services Agency (CBSA) and Ding Ding was deported to China. Her story detailed how she was not trafficked but chose to work in massage parlours because she wanted to contribute to society and provide for her children. The second story detailed how 'Niki' was robbed by a client and was scared to call the police. Eventually her friend called the police, but they did not investigate the robbery. Instead, they reported Niki to CBSA and she was subsequently deported. The narratives of both women focused on not becoming a 'burden' to society and wanting to provide for their children and family. In the story, Niki specifically mentioned her desire to 'contribute to society' through her work.

The participants on my table included a lawyer, two women from sexual health services, and a support worker from a community centre. Both the lawyer and I were aware of the Access T.O. legislation whereas the frontline workers were not. As we were discussing the stories the support worker mentioned how she had a system of 'warm transfers' where she ensured she referred precaritised clients to someone she knew. She explained how a shadow network of service providers existed to support precaritised residents despite not being able to account for this work in their targets or funding reports. This indicates the problem of illegibility that arises when services are conditioned on citizenship rather than residence and how service providers find ways to work around these challenges on the ground (see Chapter 4). She explained that providing services to precaritised residents really rests on the culture of the organisation and whether managers allowed it.

Hazel asked each table to summarise their discussion for the group and the support worker shared this practice. There seemed to be murmurs of agreement when she talked about the system of 'warm transfers'. A service provider from another table agreed and added that it has got more difficult to help these clients in the past two years because of the cuts to legal aid and therefore there are fewer legal advice centres to refer to. Another service provider then added that she has stopped providing housing support because 'it is a waste of time' as there is no affordable accommodation available. After the discussion an activist from Montreal discussed the red umbrella campaign to break down the stigma of sex work. Towards the end of the session there was the feeling that the weekend was approaching as people started leaving early. Hazel encouraged the whole room to chant 'blow jobs are jobs' which we all did quite enthusiastically before we all made our way back out onto Spadina Road.

Overall, while these are three different types of meeting, some similar processes emerge. First, migrant scapegoating had effects in each city. Media narratives based on national government fearmongering that precaritised residents drained tax revenues, were dangerous criminals or part of trafficking networks affected how municipal government could talk about the sanctuary city. However, whereas Sheffield and Toronto were largely silent, San

Francisco became more vocal, heralding the city's sanctuary status as a 'moral compass for the world' (see Chapter 5).[4] These differences indicate that while underlying processes may be similar, the way they play out is dependent on different situated and embedded contexts.

Second, spatialisation of precaritised residents in downscaled areas of the city which were then targeted in similar ways sheds light on the links between the governance of the urban poor with the governance of irregularised migrants in the three cities. In San Francisco, sanctuary city organising was shifting to encompass evictions as well as deportations to build broader solidarity within affected communities. In Sheffield, migrant organising remained largely separated from other forms of organising. In contrast to San Francisco where organising was localised in small geographical areas, migrant organising in Sheffield was located in the centre of the city, not in the places where precaritised residents lived. In Toronto, service providers in these downscaled areas had developed informal bureaucratic networks to support precaritised residents but entry to them relied on luck and being referred by an understanding and informed frontline worker.

Third, the fraught relationship between national and municipal government emerges in each vignette as national government frustrated the work of urban sanctuary actors. Federal government threatened to cut funding to San Francisco if it didn't cooperate with immigration enforcement. In Sheffield, where the city already cooperates with immigration enforcement, national government tried to embed itself further into community organisations, restricting their room for manoeuvre. First, the national government dramatically cut resources to municipal government and then offered targeted programmes of support that fulfilled their own objectives. In Toronto, national anti-trafficking policies took precedence over the Access T.O. Ordinance. By-law enforcement officers detained and deported migrant sex workers justifying their actions through the narratives of 'vulnerability' and 'rescue'.

Finally, these three meetings indicate how the sanctuary city policy was not 'fixed' but was continually undergoing a process of negotiation about common meanings and definitions. For example, Hazel tried to enrol service providers into extending their notions of belonging to include precaritised migrant sex workers. This co-option culminated in her invocation for everyone to chant 'blow jobs are jobs!' focusing on the notion of contribution through work as a route to belong. Similarly, Mei-Ying was 'translating' sanctuary city policy to Chinatown residents to link histories of Chinese exclusion and racism to contemporary criminalisation and deportation. In Sheffield, service providers debated whether sanctuary should be linked to non-cooperation with the Home Office. Meetings and trainings such as those described above were extremely rich ethnographic sites as they exemplified how policies themselves change as they enter into relations with other actors, objects, and institutions and have effects as they move through social worlds (Mosse and Lewis 2006, 14).[5]

Final Remarks

Each city had distinct differences in the way sanctuary city policy took shape. These differences are dependent upon many factors as will be developed further in the rest of the book including the type of governing system (unitary or federal); the welfare state context; the ability of the city to raise its own funds; the location of the city in global, national, and local economies; the political environment of the nation, region, and city and histories of cooperation in practice; the demographics and histories of the migrant population; the histories of organising in the city; the funding landscape; and density of non-governmental and not-for-profit organising.

However, despite these differences all the discussions pivoted on expanding who is considered to belong and on what terms. At the YMCA in San Francisco activists tried to challenge residents' notions of who belongs and asked open questions regarding why residents thought someone who has been convicted of a crime (however minor) should be deported. Sanctuary city activists challenged residents to consider what might be considered 'fair' treatment and why. At the Town Hall in Sheffield, not-for-profit organisations at the migrant forum chaired by City of Sanctuary Sheffield, debated whether asylum seekers who had exhausted appeal rights 'belong' to the city or whether they should cooperate with national government to facilitate their deportation or 'assisted return'. In Toronto, migrant activists tried to break down stigma related to sex work, politicised the language of 'rescue' and persuaded service providers to offer sex workers the same terms of belonging as other precaritised residents through appealing to their 'sense of justice'.

These events reveal important points about sanctuary city policy. We can see how sanctuary city policy is imagined in each of these moments by both activists and those they are trying to persuade. These imaginaries are also moving through time and space and have been reformulated in the present to suit a particular audience with a particular objective. In this sense the sanctuary city policy is a set of contested narratives which define the problems of the present in such a way as to either condemn or condone the past and project a viable pathway to resolution, namely a particular understanding of the way sanctuary city policy should be understood and practised. We can also see, in Clarke and colleagues' words, that policy 'is not just imagined, it is also *performed*' (2015, 30; emphasis in original). Policy is presented to real or imagined audiences, attempting to make specific proposals or projects appear as if they are logical, innovative, necessary, and obvious.[6] Policy shapes and is shaped by the context that it travels through as it is taken up in different ways in written documents, action plans, training sessions, forums, and implemented in practice. In the process, policy is both made and made meaningful in performance. These moments are instances where sanctuary becomes real.

In addition, those who make, write and implement policies are emplaced and embodied actors (Shore et al. 2011, 18).[7] Taken together, these three events show how sanctuary policy acts on and through the agency and subjectivity of actors. Through their actions and the way that the sanctuary city can take such different shapes we can see the importance of tracing the moral values around the sanctuary city and how they are negotiated.

These events also show how sanctuary city policy crystallised terms of reference and disallowed alternatives. Sanctuary city policy became the dominant discourse through which to advance a political agenda that concerned precaritised residents in each of these cities and gave institutional authority to a number of overlapping discourses. Tracing the semantic shifts in sanctuary city policy shows how it has taken on different meanings (Humphris 2020a, 2020b, 2021). In Shore and Wright's words, these semantic shifts provide 'fingerprints' for tracing more profound transformations in rationalities of governance (1997: 14). When a word or phrase such as the 'sanctuary city' succeeds both in the 'political field' and also in attracting mass popular support, Shore and Wright term them 'mobilizing metaphors'.

But why did the sanctuary city become a mobilising metaphor? How, among many competing narratives, did the notion of the sanctuary city 'succeed'? As this chapter has shown, the sanctuary city is a malleable term that can be immediately recognised but can mean many different things. The sanctuary city was effective precisely because it articulates and incorporates 'different subjects, different identities, different projects, different aspirations' into a single configuration (Hall 1988, 166). This capacity of the sanctuary city makes it useful to (fleetingly) solve fundamental tensions in governing. To understand these tensions and their common roots we need historical contextualisation. The next chapter turns to the formation of municipalities, how they were subsumed into nation-states, and the moral underpinnings that determined membership of those communities.

TWO

Tracing Sanctuary
Histories of Empire and Urban Sovereignty

> The Clerk's department is built off the British model. My experience of clerks is they are the defenders of democracy at the municipal level and were key to getting the Access T.O. ordinance through.
>
> Andrew, Director of Municipal Services, City of Toronto

This quote from Andrew indicates a key aspect linking the three sanctuary cities at the heart of this book. The history of the formation of modern municipal government explains the shared city-level bureaucratic systems in the three countries through a council, elections and wards which are represented by elected Supervisors (San Francisco) or Councillors (Sheffield and Toronto) and overseen by a Clerk of the Council. In each city the Clerk was key to ensuring implementation of sanctuary city policies. More importantly, however, tracing the entwined colonial legacies of these three cities reveals underlying logics that fundamentally shaped the relationship between the nation-state and the city. Understanding this relationship is fundamental to understanding sanctuary cities.

This history provides an alternative starting point through which to explore sanctuary cities with broad implications. Important sanctuary scholarship portrays its history through tracing its roots from early Christianity[1] and the contemporary relationship between 'the church' and 'the state'. Bagelman, among many others, provides a detailed account of how religious imagery and symbolism infuse sanctuary with the notion of a sacred and enclosed physical space (2016, 22–24, 54–56; see also Bau 1985; Coutin 1993; Cunningham 1995). This history of sanctuary also denotes safety and the power and sovereignty of the church to keep people in a designated space without fear of removal. When sanctuary scholarship shifted to sanctuary cities, rather than sanctuary movements (Humphris 2020a, 2020b, 2021), this notion of sanctuary as a defined autonomous space was transposed to the city. Some sanctuary city scholarship holds an implicit normative assumption that the city can and should maintain an autonomous space of protection for migrants from hostile nation-states.

I build on this literature by beginning from a different starting point. This chapter foregrounds how the ability to enter, remain in, or be removed from a given city has its own history and legacies that are crucial to the meaning of contemporary sanctuary cities. This history pinpoints the unbalance or the 'cracking open' that sanctuary cities represent. As will be shown below, sanctuary cities relate directly to the core purpose of cities within nation-states to contain the tension between central authority and local autonomy (Isin 1992, 154). This insight helps to reformulate a recurring question about sanctuary cities. We should not ask whether cities can act autonomously but rather what specific kinds of governing rights and obligations cities possess, for what purposes, and who is invested with these powers.

The chapter traces the history of the city as a corporation drawing out the links and circulations between urban bureaucracy in England and the formation of cities in British colonies on the Atlantic coast of North America during the seventeenth and eighteenth centuries. The aim of this chapter is to ensure that my approach to sanctuary cities does not rely on an abstract and ahistorical conception of the city that obfuscates the colonial and racial structures that pattern contemporary metropolitan governance.[2]

Focusing on the city in a historical perspective enables several theoretical interventions that link sanctuary cities to the broader stakes involved in contemporary migration, citizenship, and urban governance. First, this perspective links sanctuary cities to what has now been termed 'neocolonialism' (Spivak 1991, 220). Neocolonialism conceptualises race, gender, and class as historically re-inscribed[3] in the colonial encounter, which structured 'native' societies around the naturalisation of gendered and class hierarchies and in which the poor and racialised[4] were infantilised and deemed 'naturally' at a lower stage of civilisation. Neocolonial perspectives argue that these hierarchies remain chiefly relevant today as a principle reproducing global inequality between the wealthier, largely white Global North and the poorer, global majority of the Global South (Bhattacharyya 2018; Hanieh 2019; Winant 2004). It is this continuing reproduction of inequality (albeit in infinitely variable ways) that has led scholars such as Andrea Ritchie (2020) to term the global governance of migration a primary mode through which contemporary racial hierarchies are sustained. This chapter situates sanctuary cities within this global context, not as a new phenomenon that emerged out of social movements in the 1980s, which became incorporated into a technology of city governance, but inextricably linked to legacies of how technologies of government regulate the relationship between population, territory, and wealth.

Second, this chapter contributes to the ongoing project of, in Chakrabarty's words, 'provincializing' cities by squarely framing them within the colony-metropole nexus as one of the foundational processes of past and contemporary global inequalities (2000). The mutual connections and intersections between colony and metropole as the primary example of policy movement and mutation are fundamental to understand the key dynamics of contemporary urban governance in its treatment of 'Others'. Not only because expulsions, mass deportations and enslavements took on new deathly consequences through colonisation but also because colonies functioned as laboratories of governance, as sites for experimenting with ruling strategies and techniques, with a view to improving the art of governing in the metropole (Comaroff 1998; Cooper and Stoler 1997; Rabinow 1989; Shilliam 2018; Wright 1991). Global cities should be conceptualised as part of an ongoing imperial terrain (Danewid 2020; McClintock 1995; Stoler 1989). At a very basic level, this helps to explain the resonances between the three cities in this book in the way municipal governance is organised; how public and private space is conceptualised and controlled for example, in laws of trespass; and common aims and practices in public education, health, and policing. This perspective also adds so much more to our understanding of the common moralities that infuse these cities, including who is considered 'undesirable' or 'dangerous' and why, what constitutes 'legitimate' treatment, and notions of 'justice', who deserves it and on what terms. Focusing attention on how Britain governed its colonies allows deeper understanding of the common tensions that shape contemporary sanctuary cities, why certain arguments based on emergent moral values for sanctuary hold more weight than others, and the historical racial, gender, and class formations underpinning these processes.[5]

Third, the historical development of cities charts how it wasn't until the seventeenth century that cities lost control of determining who could enter and reside within their jurisdiction (a process that is still unfolding) (Isin 2002; Prak 2018). How cities came to be incorporated from the seventeenth to the eighteenth centuries into the nation-state sheds light on the tension in urban governance and how the city became a mode of governance through which to manage the tension of local autonomy (from below) and central authority (from above).

Moreover, there was a fundamental shift in the location of power in the move from pre-modern city-states to nation-states. Practices earlier mediated by personalised relations and by a redistributive ethic appeared to have been placed 'outside the play of local relations' (Mitchell 1991, 78). Given the advent of capitalism and the emergence of a modern state, power now appeared to emanate from somewhere beyond. In the modern state, even though power was still exercised locally and felt with immediate effect, power relations now appeared fixed and permanent rather than being localised, personalised, and fluctuating. The nation-state (despite its inherent contradictions, inconsistencies, and tensions) was seen as logical, rational, and all-powerful.

The rise of modern statehood and market economy signifies at the same time a subordination of the city to the nation as the only sovereign political community (Magnusson 1996). Moreover, Mignolo has shown that the rise of modern states and coloniality were two aspects of the same development in different forms of power (2003). Critical race scholars pinpoint that in the making of colonialism on which capitalism relied, strategies of urban regeneration, slum administration, and law and order policing emerged. This scholarship helps to bridge pre-modern urban concerns about sanitation, plague, crime, and disorder with colonial urban governance (Goldberg 2002). The resonances of these urban governance policies can be traced to current contemporary urban moral values of the 'efficient', 'healthy', and 'just' city that make up the contemporary sanctuary cities addressed in Chapter 4.

These three cities are linked through their shared colonial histories. Britain's changing ideas about how to organise the relationship between population and territory for the strength and wealth of the nation shifted through the experience of governing colonies in North America. One way to frame the relation between population, territory, and wealth is to think about the ongoing reconciliation of the desire for a large, cheap, flexible, and compliant labour force to satisfy economic demands with the desire to minimise any perceived social and economic costs. These economic concerns had significant moral dimensions linked to who deserved to be present in a given territory. The reconciliation of this tension is playing out as much in the formation of the first modern urban conurbations as in debates about sanctuary cities today. These common threads show that these forms of government are not self-evident. By shedding new light on how urban sanctuary governance inheres from a particular history and through excavating the underlying justifications of sanctuary governance we can ask different questions and open realms of alternative possibilities.

Transformations in Government and Politics

We can trace the circulation of ideas between colony and metropole from the foundations of settlement in British colonies in North America. First, in the late seventeenth century there was a move from plantations, which were seen as possessions, towards towns which had to be governed. British colonial administration formulated the connection between population, territory, and wealth very clearly as opposed to the French, Dutch, Spanish, and Portuguese in the Americas (Isin 2002, 179–181; Prak 2018, 282–284).[6] Britain's strategies of settlement became increasingly elaborate. Systematic land settlement through building towns was the instrument of bringing more people into the regulated orbit of governance and thus of the generation of wealth and stability (Isin 1992, 68). Moreover, in 1773 the Enclosure Act explicitly referred to the plantation economies of the Americas. The 'problem' of England's rural poor was being apprehended in terms of African enslavement and allowed common lands to be cultivated, 'improved', and regulated (Shilliam 2018, 19–30).

Legal and political thought circulated between colony and metropole to address the dilemmas of governing colonies 'at a distance'.[7] From the seventeenth century until the US Declaration of Independence various inventions in colonial apparatus and new governing institutions were developed[8] (Isin 1992, 184–191). The most crucial was the realisation that allegiance had to be inculcated through direct governance (Isin 1992, 140–175 and 2002, 184–189). This realisation led to the creation of the 'incorporated city' which determines the political relationship between city and nation-state to this day. The incorporated city rests on the principle that the corporation is distinct from its residents (thus residents are not vested with any rights as citizens). It is the city governing body that is vested with rights and obligations (but only those powers that are explicitly granted by nation-state legislature) (Isin 1992, 2).

Without cities as 'close corporations' British Parliament believed it was impossible to govern territories from afar because colonial governors practised considerable judgement if not autonomy. 'Close corporations' were *de jure* cities that had been created by royal charter, had royally appointed governors, and most resembled English early modern cities. In contrast, corporate colonies organised their towns in accordance with their own needs and dictates of local politics and culture. The failure to subjugate *de facto* corporations was seen as one reason for rebellions (Isin 1992, 10–11).[9]

Following the rebellions of Upper and Lower Canada (Toronto and Montreal) in 1837 and 1838[10] there was realisation that direct centralised power polarised opposition. Local authorities were needed to allow city residents to participate in their own government. The principles of incorporation and systems of municipal governance, elections, and representation were instituted through British colonial governance[11] (Isin and Wood 1999, 153). With this subjugated relationship to the modern nation-state, cities also gained a new franchise relationship. Cities were considered a legal and political institution with 'explicit delegated powers and liabilities to undertake the governance of citizens of the state' (Isin 1992, 57). On one hand the city as a municipal corporation exercised power authorised by the state. On the other, *some* residents of the city authorise the governing body to act on its behalf within the powers prescribed (Isin 1992, 16–55).

A further legacy of the new municipal corporations was the rise of new professions which constituted the building, regulating, and monitoring of the city as their fields of expertise.[12] These professions emerged from Britain's objective to 'provide good order and government and prevent vice' (Isin 1992, 167). As Home illustrates, colonial agents in their increasingly professional capacities and identities left an indelible mark on the city (1997, 37). Early municipal corporations pioneered technologies such as public health, public education, city planning, and later social work which became 'precise fields of governance'.[13] Crucially, through the incorporation of cities into municipal corporations, nation-states could use cities as an apparatus of governance. Indeed, Isin argues this is the sole reason that colonial cities were incorporated at all, to ensure more efficient and effective governance of the colonies by diffusing power and penetrating new societies (1992, 174). Just as in England, municipal corporations in the colonies were actively used by national governments to administer legislation, primarily expressed through the Poor

Laws. City governance therefore had direct consequences for the governance of mobile poor. Commonalities across cities emerged in the distinctions between deserving and undeserving poor based on the economic concerns of the new municipalities subsumed under nation-states.

Governing Urban 'Undesirables' in Incorporated Municipalities

As reviewed above, ideas to advance the wealth and strength of the British nation-state provided the impetus for concentrations of labour leading to town planting and later the rise of municipal corporations in the colonies. These ideas were entwined with significant moral dimensions which ordered who deserved to be present in the municipality and under what conditions. Well-documented systems of forced movement abounded from the foundation of the colonies.[14] Indigenous peoples were exterminated (Saunt 2020), while Britain forcibly moved people to the thirteen colonies for labour through large-scale programmes of removal, transportation, indentured labour, and enslavement (Davis 2006; Hirota 2016; Kanstroom 2007; Palmer 1998). Similar catastrophic processes were evident in Upper and Lower Canada (see Winks 2008 for overview).[15] The remainder of this chapter traces the limited topic of how colonial systems of municipal governance developed to mark out the deserving from undeserving poor and how this shifted as cities became an apparatus of government subsumed within nation-states.

Historical scholarship attests that a culture of excluding 'nonproducing members' from society with racialised underpinnings in British colonies in North America was evident as early as 1634 (Kanstroom 2007, 34–39).[16] Debate on governing the poor in British colonies drew on the sixteenth century British Poor Law tradition (Midgley 2011) and made a significant impact on the design of institutional frameworks in the late seventeenth and eighteenth centuries (Prak 2018, 290).[17] The British Poor Laws were an instrument of non-contributory poor relief based on residence (Midgley 1984; Seekings 2013).[18] Alongside the Poor Laws, workhouses were used for 'promoting and inculcating principles and habits of industry and moral virtue' (Isin 1989, 24). In addition, police wardens were assigned to control 'idleness' and 'drunkenness' reporting to the Board of Police, and health wardens were assigned to control 'cleanliness' reporting to the Board of Health' (Isin 1992, 51).[19] The first workhouse in the colonies was purchased by New York City municipality and opened its doors in 1701. It represented the beginning of the gradual introduction of English institutions into the formerly Dutch colony (Prak 2018, 288). During the eighteenth century the colonies followed the English trend as public welfare shifted away from church provision to incorporated municipal authorities (Prak 2018, 289).

Several other tools were developed to govern 'undesirable' or 'non-productive' residents in the early colonies. New England towns established a 'warning out' system that allowed them to remove residents who had been reduced to poverty or for any other reason deemed socially objectionable such as having a baby or trespass (Zuckerman 1970, 112–113).[20] Police constables were paid for the bodily removal of 'undesirables' from incorporated towns (Kanstroom 2007, 91; Zuckerman 1970, 113).

With America's Declaration of Independence in 1776, colonists perpetuated liberal aspects of their colonial pasts. The transient poor continued to be particularly demonised, perceived as refusing to participate in production due to moral failings.[21] By the nineteenth century, urban poverty was problematised from three directions. First, fears the poor would avail themselves on the city and would incur interminable economic costs. Second, spaces of urban poverty were portrayed as hotbeds for disease and breeding grounds for crime.[22] Third, the urban poor were 'visible signs of the social failures that accompanied the rise of urban industrial society' (Schweik 2009, 165). They were deemed 'unsightly' and an affront to the emerging sensibilities of urban residents. Racial theories of social deviance and fears of miscegenation also became a prominent lens through which to look at the increasingly devastating socio-economic and sanitary conditions of the urban poor (Smith 2013). These concerns around health, safety, efficiency, and justice can be conceived as stemming from the desire for order and predictability that has been a concern of city administrations from their foundation (Isin 1999; Bauman 1999; Dürr et al. 2020; Katz 1997).

Many cities included proscriptive clauses in their laws to discourage immigration of 'undesirable aliens' and to limit the rights of 'unproductive' naturalised citizens (Baseler 1998, 220). Similar to 'warning out' systems for paupers, cities instituted regulations deeming that anyone unlikely to be able to take care of themselves were screened and refused entry including, but not limited to, those considered to be 'blind, idiotic, crippled, epileptic, lunatic, or other infirm foreign pauper' (Law 2014). The contemporary notions of deservingness for both 'failed citizens' and 'non-citizens' have a shared history

that can be traced back to these early fears of the economic costs of 'non-pro-
ducing members' for incorporated municipalities (Anderson 2013). Little difference was made between itinerant paupers from within the nation-state or
from outside. However, during the nineteenth century the nation-state and
geo-political national border assumed primary control over population movement. In essence, the nation-state, not the city, now decided who belonged, on
what terms, and why. The following section traces this shift in each pioneering sanctuary city.

Cities Losing Sovereignty

San Francisco

In 1850, California became the 31st state and followed a remarkably similar
approach to the Atlantic seaboard states in its approach to itinerant paupers.
San Francisco was the first American city to pass an 'Ugly Law' in 1867, in
the aftermath of the Gold Rush when many unemployed internal and foreign
migrants were visibly poor in the city (Schweik 2009). California passed a similar law five years later. The frame for the California Ugly Law was based on
all those who did not have settlement in the state. No distinction was made
between foreign migrants or internal itinerants.

Shortly after the incorporation of California into the Union in 1850, it
introduced immigrant taxes for the first time. The 1852 Passenger Act was
largely based on similar laws that had been passed on Atlantic coastal states.[23]
It required shipmasters to provide a bond of $500 or pay $5 in head money to
the state of California or the entry of each passenger. Similarly to the Atlantic coastal states, and immigrant taxes in Upper and Lower Canada, the Act
banned the landing of 'any lunatic, idiot, deaf, dumb, blind, crippled or infirm
person' as well as any person who had been a pauper in any other country and
who appeared to be likely to become a public charge 'from sickness or disease'
(Baseler 1998, 197–198).

The Act established a Commissioner of Emigration for the city of San Francisco, authorising the official to implement the Act's provisions (Kanazawa
2005, 786). California not only targeted the poor but also racially targeted Chinese migrants who were seen as threatening 'the most vital interests of the
State and the people' due to successful gold mining (Kanazawa 2005, 783).[24]
California's legislature tried to exclude all non-European foreigners either
through landing taxes or foreign miners' taxes (Hirota 2017, 89). At the same

time California was also purging the mining industry of Indigenous Americans, people of Mexican descent who resided in California before it became part of the United States, and Latin Americans (Smith 2013, 82).[25] However, every legislative attempt to restrict immigration suffered legal constraints due to its clash with federal authority. It is important to note that the tension was not due to a moral indictment but an economic concern over control of foreign commerce.

Until the mid-nineteenth century the control of immigration was seen largely as a matter of California's police power (Kanstroom 2007, 92). Promoting foreign commerce was the impetus for federal authority to take precedence, for example in the Supreme Court ruling invalidating New York's immigrant 'head tax' and the overruling of San Francisco's tax on miners and Chinese laundries. It was not until 1875 that Congress passed a federal statute dealing with immigrants' entry.[26] Consequently, state legislations limiting the entry of aliens were deemed to be pre-empted by federal statute and the federal government began making arguments solely based on inherent sovereign powers (not on foreign commerce clauses). Lacking an express constitutional clause conferring the power to the Congress, the Supreme Court stated that the regulation of the entry and the stay of aliens in the national territory was 'an incident of sovereignty belonging to the government of the U.S.'. This statute signalled the end of sub-federal control of immigration and is the origin of the logic that still governs today.

Sheffield

Similar laws were implemented in the metropole to control local autonomy. Sheffield was not fully subsumed as an apparatus of government in the English nation-state until 1842. Before 1842, power was dispersed between three historic institutions: the Church Burgesses, Cutlers' Company, and the Town Trustees (Price 2011, 9). Sheffield gained a reputation for being a centre of revolutionary politics due to its lack of centralised power, radical religious nonconformists, and militant artisans. National government increasingly tried to bring it under centralised control.[27] After an uprising in 1791, Parliament continuously quartered troops in Sheffield and a barracks was built in the city to house them. As a result of the Reform Act in 1832, some Sheffield residents[28] could elect two Members of Parliament with the aim of quietening discontent. In 1842, Sheffield became incorporated as a town under the control of Whitehall and instituted a town council (Price 2011, 38). Sheffield became fully constituted as an integral part of a system of nation-state governance subsumed under the control of the British Parliament.

Before 1842, national government consistently intervened in city governance to establish central authority over local control. A key development occurred regarding the regulations of guilds. In Sheffield, any person born outside Hallamshire (the historical name for the area surrounding Sheffield) was considered to be a 'foreigner'. No distinction was made between those who crossed a national border and those from another town or city in England. Sheffield artisans feared lowered wages due to the influx of cheap labour of 'foreigners'. Parliament intervened in 1814 and removed regulations on the entry into the professions[29] ceasing local control of regulating newcomers to the city.

A further turning point in the removal of local autonomy was through the Poor Law Amendment Act of 1834 (the Act). Sheffield had implemented its own system of the Poor Laws since the sixteenth century. Local 'Overseers of the Poor' collected local rates and supported the poor mostly through 'outdoor relief' rather than workhouses. The Act provoked outcry and protest because it ceased outdoor relief in favour of workhouses. Moreover, it instituted national, rather than local, enforcement of Poor Laws. The City's Overseers were replaced by two new Poor Law Unions of Guardians who continued outdoor relief but were national government representatives, and not under the control of the city. This marks the end of local control of poor relief. However, while poor relief was governed nationally, access to relief continued to be conditioned on municipal residence and not national citizenship. As in Canada and the USA, Poor Laws were the underpinnings of modern day welfare states. Until the 1970s, eligibility for welfare was determined on urban residence rather than formal citizenship. This opening allowed municipalities to retain some form of local autonomy to determine who could access welfare within their jurisdiction free from federal control. As we shall see in the next chapter, that opening has closed as national governments entwine immigration and welfare regulations provoking what scholars now call inland border enforcement or 'everyday bordering' (Yuval-Davis et al. 2018).

Toronto

In Canada, provinces had passed statutes regulating immigration based on the English Poor Law tradition. They forbid entry to those who could become a burden upon local welfare or had been previously convicted of crimes elsewhere. This applied to internal itinerants and foreign migrants. Toronto, two years after its incorporation as a city in 1834, adopted many measures taken directly from England to discipline and inculcate 'useful' habits in its urban poor. 'Houses of industry' were established with the aim of abolishing begging and vagrants alongside other institutions transposed from England including penitentiaries, asylums, prisons, and schools with the expressed aim of improving 'the community at large' through disciplining to guard against idleness and habits of vice and immorality (Isin 1992, 147). Immigrant taxes were also in operation in Lower and Upper Canada, transposed from New York and Massachusetts (Kelley and Trebilcock 2000, 51).

The Canadian Constitution Act of 1867 heralded immigration as a concurrent jurisdiction between federal government and the provinces; however, it granted federal Parliament wide discretion in defining the role of the provinces in immigration (Strazzari 2017, 63). Soon after the Constitution Act the provinces agreed that federal Parliament would comprehensively deal with immigration. The Immigration Act 1869, the first federal statute on immigration, was heavily influenced by provincial statutes and was similarly aimed at deterring the entry of specific classes of immigrants deemed dangerous for public order or likely to become a burden on public welfare. These Acts signalled the end of provincial control over who could enter or remain in their jurisdiction. They also represent the crystallisation of the importance of national origin to formal citizenship. However, social citizenship and access to social assistance remained dependent on notions of residence, not formal citizenship status, until the mid-twentieth century similar to the US and UK.

Final Remarks

This chapter demonstrates how models of urban citizenship in the British metropolis exerted powerful influence on citizenship arrangements and governing institutions implemented in the colonies. The circulations of colonial ideas and practices set in motion ways of thinking about the relation between population, territory, and wealth and how to govern the resulting urban formations, which still reverberates through contemporary cities.

First, the changes in Britain provided the key concepts in political and legal discourse about the city that formed part of the British colonial apparatus. With the development of liberalism as a programme of nation-state

administration in England, coupled with rapidly changing colonial conditions, a new series of colonial policies emerged which constituted the
city in modern political and legal terms as an apparatus of governance. As
highlighted in the introduction, this line of inquiry helps to pinpoint the
unbalance or the 'cracking open' that sanctuary cities represent. It relates
directly to the core purpose of cities within nation-states to contain the
tension between central authority and local autonomy (Isin 1992, 154). It
has traced the changing governing rights and obligations cities possess, for
what purposes, and who was invested with these powers. In addition, this
chapter introduced the importance of intermediary institutions of states
and provinces, not least for their capacity to disrupt the relationship between the city and the nation-state. As will become clear through comparison between the cities in the following chapters, federalism provides
sanctuary actors in San Francisco and Toronto with room for manoeuvre,
while in Sheffield sanctuary actors are exposed to a central and centralising nation-state.

Second, this chapter marks the time period when immigration became
a federal government concern and not within the jurisdiction of cities or
states.[30] Colonial towns in the seventeenth and eighteenth century retained
the right to accept only those that they wished and often did not discriminate
between 'undesirables' from another political community in the thirteen
colonies or abroad (Zuckerman 1970, 110–111). As described above, during the
eighteenth and nineteenth centuries many states enacted statutes with the
aim of deterring the entry of 'paupers, idiots, lunatics and aliens', usually
by imposing levies on shipmasters (Motomura 2014, 65). The constitutional
authority to enact statutes in the United States and in Canada was based on
the police powers of the states and on English Poor Law tradition (Trattner
1989).[31] State and provincial immigration policies sat in uneasy tension with
federal power (Kanstroom 2007; Zolberg 2009). By the end of the nineteenth
century, federal government had assumed supremacy over immigration
matters in both the United States and Canada as enshrined in the constitutions of both of those nation-states.

While federal government gained supremacy over immigration regulations in the US, internal governance of paupers and relief agencies eligibility

criteria continued to be based on need and county residence, not federal citizenship (Fox 2012).[32] A similar system was evident in Canada and the UK.[33] State Poor Laws and their residence requirements rather than federal alienage-based restrictions marked the boundaries of social citizenship until the 1970s when the latter took primacy (Fox 2016, 1056). The next chapter details the extent to which formal citizenship and national government has come to increasingly determine access to welfare and social citizenship and the concomitant effects for urban governance.

THREE

Emplacing Sanctuary
Hierarchies of Authority and Enforcement

> I tell them, you don't have the papers to prove it officially, but you are a resident. Residency means that you live in the place. This is what gave me peace of mind when I was undocumented. But you need someone to tell you. That's what we're trying to do.
>
> Camila, Toronto sanctuary activist

To understand sanctuary cities, we must place each city within its national legal constitution and policy context. I introduce the idea of 'hierarchies of enforcement' to help identify trends between cities. I define these hierarchies as whether formal national citizenship or city residence takes precedence in decided eligibility for services. In essence, whether precaritised residents can access services based on living in the city, or whether they need legal status. In addition, as alluded to by the quote from Camila, the chapter also explores the practices developed by activists to help precaritised residents navigate city services.

The chapter details four key issues shaping sanctuary practices in each city. First, it describes the extent to which cities can control migration policy within their legal constitutions. Second, it explores direct immigration enforcement. Third, the chapter moves on to how immigration control was implicitly constructed through rules and regulations that require forms of proof, validation or identification, how those services were funded, and how gatekeepers were trained. Finally, the chapter illustrates the role of fear as a bordering mechanism and municipal responses.

Legal Constitution of Cities
The legal constitution of the municipality within the nation-state is a key determinant of whether the city can diverge from national immigration and

settlement policy. In San Francisco, the most important element of the legal constitution is the city's status as a city and a county.[1] There is a fundamental distinction between a county and a city. The state legislature may delegate to the counties any of the functions that belong to the state. As Abigail, the deputy director of the Human Services Agency (HSA), explained:

> California is somewhat unique because county agencies administer funds. In other states, states have offices in the city and administer programs. Even if they were a sanctuary city, they would not have any way to extend the sanctuary policy to the administration of welfare benefits. So that's something that we are able to do because we are a city and a county.

The California Constitution recognises two types of counties: general law counties and charter counties. San Francisco is one of fourteen charter counties. Charter counties are afforded a governing structure that allows for greater local control. By adopting and amending a charter, county voters can take advantage of constitutional discretion over the county's governing board, officers, and employees (see Long 1911). In practice, this means that San Francisco can make ordinances, such as the City of Refuge Ordinance that was passed in 1985.

The extent to which San Francisco's legal constitution allows for divergence from national policy has been widely debated by constitutional lawyers for decades, and particularly since the most recent challenges to 'sanctuary jurisdictions' by the Trump administration.[2] As traced in the previous chapter, before the Civil War, states and counties had full control over immigration laws. After the outlawing of slavery, the federal government became the dominant locus of immigration power.[3] Due to the resurgence in state and county attempts to control immigration, the term 'the new immigration federalism' has been used to explain sub-federal immigration policy-making. Legal scholars have analysed the role that state and local governments doctrinally and normatively play in the regulation and enforcement of immigration law[4] and the constitutionality of 'sanctuary cities'.[5] They have also identified how local laws can just as easily be detrimental to progressive migration policies as support them.[6] The primary constitutional argument for sanctuary cities is based on the Tenth Amendment guarantee of freedom from federal commandeering of local resources. Immigration and Customs Enforcement (ICE) detainers have also been challenged on Fourth Amendment principles that guarantee individuals cannot be held against their will without a judicial warrant or probable cause (Lasch et al. 2018).

The position of municipalities in the UK is very different. The UK is a unitary government and therefore devolves very few powers to local authorities. Since 2016, municipalities have been able to elect their own mayors.[7] Sheffield is part of the Sheffield City Region (which combines Barnsley, Doncaster, Rotherham, and Sheffield Combined Authority) that took up this affordance and elected its first regional Mayor in May 2018. However, the elected mayors hold no power over migration or criminal justice issues; rather they focus on regional transport, skills training, and economic development.

Since 2012, the UK national government has had an explicit policy of creating a 'hostile environment' for migrants (switching name but not content to compliant environment' in 2018).[8] In practice, this has meant increasing internal migration status checks within everyday life and devolving the responsibility to check migration status to governmental and non-governmental actors. The pervasive nature of immigration control into all aspects of life has been termed 'everyday bordering' by migration scholars (Yuval-Davis et al. 2019).

A limited number of local authorities in England have not cooperated with national government, such as not sharing data with the Home Office on non-citizen homeless rough sleepers[9] or refusing to embed Home Office staff in local government or police departments (Siddons and McIntyre 2018; Busby 2019). While these responses do not amount to local municipalities' control over migration, it is notable that Sheffield has not joined either of these initiatives.

National government gives municipalities a choice whether to assume a duty of care for recognised refugees through national level programmes. For example in 2001, the then Home Secretary, David Blunkett, a Sheffield MP, advocated with the UN Refugee Agency (UNHCR) that the UK should take more refugees from refugee camps. The legal basis was established by the Nationality, Immigration and Asylum Act 2002 (NIA 2002). The resulting policy was called the 'Gateway Programme' and launched in March 2004. Sheffield was one of the first cities to welcome refugees through this programme. SCC also signed up to the Vulnerable Persons Resettlement Scheme to settle Syrian refugees (who were not already in the European Union) in January 2014 and implemented the unaccompanied asylum-seeking scheme (Dubs Amendment that was passed in 2016 but scrapped in 2017). SCC supported the programme of refugee community sponsorship and the Afghan resettlement scheme and implements national government sanctioned programmes, while refusing to engage in non-cooperation practices.

Toronto's emplacement within the nation-state is illustrated through two key events.[10] The first is Toronto's amalgamation in 1998 and the second is the Memorandum of Understanding between the federal, municipal, and city level in 2006. In 1998, the Province of Ontario consolidated Metropolitan Toronto and its six lower-tier municipalities into a single City of Toronto. It was a controversial decision. Supporters claimed amalgamation would produce a more cost-effective, transparent, and responsive local government, while opponents argued the elimination of the lower-tier municipalities would diminish the quality of democratic representation.

In Canada, municipalities are generally conceived as creatures of the provinces, with powers and responsibilities that are circumscribed by provincial legislation (Frisken 2007; Leo and Martine 2009; Tolley and Young 2011). As Clare, a Toronto City lawyer explained, 'Municipalities don't have any inherent right to exist. They are not constitutionally provided for. It's entirely up to the province and once they've established a municipality they can authorize it to do anything that they decide'. Current constitutional arrangements mandate little official involvement for municipalities in immigration and settlement policies. However, more recently, socio-legal scholars have challenged the constitutional perspective and convincingly argued that Canadian municipalities are better understood as jurisdictions that play 'an unpredictable, multiplayer, open-ended game' (Valverde 2021, 25). This understanding more accurately resonates with the way sanctuary city policy was negotiated in Toronto.

A mechanism for increased cooperation opened in September 2006, through the Canada-Ontario Immigration Agreement, COIA, which was signed with the aim to create new relationships among federal, provincial, and municipal governments through memoranda of understanding concerning the provision of settlement services. The COIA enhanced the role of the City of Toronto in intergovernmental arrangements concerning immigration and settlement.

The COIA had a number of effects on the arrangement of immigrant services in Toronto. For example, it introduced Toronto's Local Immigration Partnerships (LIP) which are 'multi-sectoral partnerships at the local level to integrate newcomer needs into the municipal planning process, while influencing provincial and federal priorities and processes' (Burr 2011, 7). While local governments lead many of the LIPs in Ontario, four of the Toronto LIPs are led by non-governmental organisations, while the City heads a fifth, city-wide LIP. These arrangements and the relationships that developed particularly between federal and municipal employees became crucial to how the sanctuary city evolved.

From this brief review, we can see how the legal constitution of each city and their approach to migration shaped room for manoeuvre on sanctuary city policy. A key distinction between the three cities is the difference between federal (Toronto and San Francisco) and unitary governing systems (Sheffield). Both Toronto and San Francisco came to utilise similar arguments based on the limitations of the city level to rationalise and justify their sanctuary city status.

First, they argued that cities did not have the policy expertise, jurisdiction or resources to address migration status. This purported 'limitation' allowed the city to diverge from federal policy. Andrew, a director of municipal services stated, 'Any discussion about who should be here, or how people might get here is not our purview. And I don't have the policy resources to start developing policy expertise in areas that aren't in the City mandate'. Similarly, in San Francisco, this 'limitation' was based on upholding the US Constitution. As Angelina, a legislative aide to a Supervisor commented, 'Everyone deserves constitutional rights regardless of their immigrant status . . . [sanctuary] ensures that the federal government doesn't use our local resources for whatever they need to do as the federal government'. Toronto and San Francisco, through invoking their limitations of authority and resources, expanded their duties towards precarious residents. Municipal officers in Sheffield did not separate their duties or aims from those of the national government.

Second, and relatedly, Toronto and San Francisco argued municipal government served all residents of the city, not only citizens, invoking eligibility first codified in the Poor Laws. In Toronto, the municipal government framed precarious residents in terms of a city obligation, not in terms of the needs of the residents. Andrew, the previous director of municipal services, stated,

> I play the City of Toronto is an incorporation of its residents. I go back to that
> every time. I will never forget the moment when I was talking with our city

solicitor and I asked, what is the definition of the City of Toronto? And she said, an incorporation of its residents. And I said, so is it fair for me to say to Council, we have a duty to care for anyone in the City. And she said, I can nod on that one if you need me to. So I could make the argument sanctuary isn't something we're doing because we're nice. This is the legislation we operate under. It's our duty to be doing this.

Municipal officers made a similar argument in San Francisco. Anthea, the director of a municipal department focusing on immigration issues and civic affairs stated, 'We serve all of the people, not just some of the people'. This argument was not evident in Sheffield. In addition, Sheffield's City of Sanctuary commitment was based on meeting needs rather than fulfilling duties.

Direct Immigration Enforcement

The second aspect of emplacing sanctuary cities is how each city responded to direct involvement of immigration officials within the city through raids and joint operations with police.[11] Immigration enforcement officers needed legal permission to enter different spaces. For example, there is a difference between public space, public transport, licensed premises or a private home or shelter. As Pablo, a doctor at Zuckerberg San Francisco Hospital described,

> In drawing up our ICE raid guidelines there was a lot of debate around public and private space—what is the sidewalk, the parking lot, the courtyard of the hospital, the waiting room, do you have to go through the doors? What parts are private for the purposes of providing sanctuary or falling under sanctuary guidelines—when do they start and stop?

However, this patchwork not only comprises different governance regimes, but also moral boundaries around different spaces governed by unspoken rules of what is seen to be 'right'. While the legal standing of conducting immigration enforcement raids across the three countries is similar (judicial warrants are required), what is different is the degree to which agencies enforce these conditions and what is morally acceptable and legitimate practice.[12]

San Francisco developed an alert system to identify immigration raids.[13] In 2008, armed immigration raids at workplaces and homes increased in the city. San Francisco Immigrant Legal & Education Network (SFILEN), funded by the San Francisco Civic Engagement & Immigrant Affairs Office, hired an attorney to handle the cases of those detained during these raids, funded by the City. They also set up the Rapid Response Network. If people saw ICE in the street, they would call the hotline. An attorney would be contacted who would try to find the detained person and represent them.

SFILEN also held trainings for organisations to distinguish between an administrative warrant (that could be denied) and a judicial warrant (that needed to be fulfilled). Almost, every organisation I visited in San Francisco volunteered their ICE raid policy. While organisations were concerned that frontline and reception staff might not feel confident enough to enact the policy, I was told that all reception staff had completed ICE raid training. Organisations also regularly ran 'Know Your Rights' training and provided details in different languages of what to do when approached by a law enforcement officer.

In Sheffield, similarly to San Francisco, immigration enforcement officers could only enter a business if they had written authorisation in the form of a warrant. Immigration officers are allowed to enter licensed premises without a warrant or written authorisation to check if people working there have the right to work. The penalties for both employees and employers who broke the law included fines of £20,000 per 'undocumented worker', a prison sentence of up to five years or both. Immigration officials could seize property or earnings or close businesses. There were no 'Know Your Rights' trainings in Sheffield or training for frontline or reception staff to distinguish between an administrative or a judicial warrant.

In Toronto, police or an immigration officer required a valid search warrant to access any public or private access area in an organisation. After several high-profile immigration raids of schools and women's shelters in 2006, causing large-scale public outcry, Canadian Border Services Agency (CBSA) changed their tactics and stopped conducting very visible raids that included children and survivors of domestic violence organisations within the city. An advocacy organisation funded by voluntary donations called No One Is Illegal (NOII) provided 'Know Your Rights' training to service providers. These trainings were only organised when NOII volunteers had capacity.

This section demonstrates the differing resources and responses to immigration raids across the three cities. It is notable that San Francisco municipal funds resource the Rapid Response Network and all immigrant-serving organisations had an ICE raid policy. During 2017, while multiple raids were taking place in the surrounding counties, there was only one ICE raid in San Francisco. In contrast, there was very little awareness or organising against immigration raids in Sheffield and, through my interviews, I came to understand that this kind of organising was not seen as part of the 'City of Sanctuary'. In Toronto, public opinion turned against CBSA when they began to conduct immigration raids in schools and women's shelters. Immigration raids took place but less visibly. Know your rights training was sporadic because it relied on voluntary work by NOII.

Domesticating Migration Policy and Inland Border Enforcement

The third aspect of emplacing sanctuary cities is tracing eligibility requirements for city services. It is important to note that it is only very recently that formal citizenship status and not local residence has become the primary determining factor for eligibility (Fox 2016). The laws and policies that now implicitly govern migration at the city level are numerous and complex. With that in mind, I have summarised the key laws and policies in Appendix 2 and devote the remainder of this chapter to exploring how they are implemented in practice, where and how data sharing might take place and with what effects for precaritised residents' lives.[14]

Police

The San Francisco Police Department (SFPD) is under the jurisdiction of the City and County of San Francisco and therefore is required to comply with section 12H of Administrative Code[15] and was updated by Chief William Scott in 2017.[16] While this policy prohibits collaboration between federal immigration enforcement and the police, community organisations reported that the police were still feared because,

> The police see it as one less thing they have to do (check immigration status) so it makes their life easier. But they still believe in the system they are working within, not transformative justice. People are still very afraid of the police. They are not there to protect us (Ah-Lam, San Francisco undocumented migrant activist).

While the SFPD have policies of non-cooperation with ICE, the underlying logics of policing remain the same, with evidence of racial profiling and intensified policing in areas that had a larger proportion of racialised residents (Mancina 2016). As Vijay, the director of a municipal service commented,

> The police have a long way to go in building a meaningful relationship with the communities they try to protect. We know there is a significant undocumented Latino community being disproportionately profiled by the police, but we are also saying come to us to report this and we will not arrest or incarcerate you. At the end of the day if you are an undocumented person living at the nexus of multiple oppressions you are not going to the police.

These comments indicate the difference between policy and practice on the ground and the pervading role of fear despite non-cooperation policies between local and federal law enforcement.

In contrast, South Yorkshire Police is not under the jurisdiction of SCC and had no formal policies or procedures for those with uncertain migration status. Unlike San Francisco and Toronto there had not been any advocacy to challenge police behaviour. Stephen, a Detective Inspector, described how immigration offences are seen as 'another string to our bow' to arrest and detain someone if there was not enough evidence to charge that person with a crime. He also explained that custody forms ask whether someone is a foreign national and if so, an immigration check is triggered. Even if the person was born in Britain, they may still undergo an immigration check. He continued, 'we have some who are born and bred in Sheffield—like Jamaicans—a number of them have been deported because they have been in our custody'. Research has also shown how the police and Home Office share databases, so police can check immigration status when they 'Stop and Search'. These policies have racialised effects. For every 'White North European' person stopped, searched, and their fingerprints scanned, twenty-eight Arabic, fourteen Black, and fourteen Asian residents are scanned[17] (Wangari-Jones et al. 2021). South Yorkshire Police also engage in joint operations with the Home Office and Stephen explained that there was a Home Office employee 'in the office every week' signalling the extent of the collaboration.

The Ontario Police Services Act governs the Toronto Police Service (TPS) and therefore the police are not under the jurisdiction of the municipality. Similarly to Sheffield, TPS have made it clear through policy interpretation and implementation that migration status overrides any other duty (Da Costa 2020; Hershkowitz et al. 2021). Unlike the other two cities, no one from TPS agreed to speak to me about the sanctuary policy. TPS had also refused to engage with advocates and Toronto City Council depositions. In 2016, a public outcry following an egregious case pushed the TPS to agree to a 'don't ask' policy but made it clear that they were still going to report anyone they knew was undocumented. The case was described to me by Drew, a NOII activist as follows,

> A 16-year-old from Grenada went to the police to report an assault against her and instead of dealing with the perpetrator, they handed her over to immigration enforcement. Her family got in touch with NOII and there was a really massive community response culminating in very aggressive confrontational rallies at Toronto Police headquarters. We got into the Toronto Police Services Board and that's where the first demands for a 'don't ask, don't tell' policy came around. The police agreed just the 'don't ask' policy. If they find information they are still going to tell.

Alongside direct collaboration between police and immigration enforcement, everyday surveillance and data collection policies have become instrumental tools throughout all three cities in identifying those without legal status, all with racialised effects. Policies such as the 'war on drugs', 'war on terror', 'broken windows' policing, and other policing practices targeting gangs, street vendors, and prostitution, as well as regulatory and traffic law enforcement, are potential sites of detention and deportation.

Housing

San Francisco housing policy allows undocumented residents to access housing support programmes provided by the city (but there is very little housing stock so in practice it is extremely difficult to access housing support). Undocumented residents cannot access permanent support in social housing because it is conditioned by federal programmes. Private landlords often require citizenship verification. Desiree, a housing provider explained, 'someone needs to have residency on the lease and sometimes that is a kid. So that is a difficult negotiation in the family. So we try and go through risk analysis of what that means for a family if they choose to put their son on the lease for example'.

Housing has also exacerbated other issues. For example, when children were being released from immigration detention facilities at the Mexican-US border to their families in San Francisco, ICE asked for the fingerprints of everyone in the household in which the child was going to reside. Hannah, child right's lawyer explained,

> They are defining household very broadly in this situation, so if you layer into this the housing crisis when everyone is living with everyone else, it makes it very difficult for families. Why in the world would an undocumented person who is not related to this child give ICE their fingerprints and have that information shared with the federal government? Maybe the mom and dad would do that but their neighbour? There is a ton of fear around sponsoring children and you are putting people at risk that maybe you don't even know very well. The housing crisis has made a real difference.

School social workers described a similar situation. Maria, a support worker in the SF Unified School District explained that social workers no longer work on housing because, 'for undocumented families I could spend months and months with one family to get housing and there's still nothing out there to give them. It's beyond anything that can be managed. One of our schools opened their gymnasium to house their families.' Lack of housing and gentrification are systemic issues that emerge in the other two cities.

In the UK, those with a precarious legal migration status were labelled 'No Recourse to Public Funds' (NRPF). There were very limited instances where local authorities can use discretionary power to provide housing to someone considered NRPF to prevent a breach of human rights (NRPF 2023). There were no government funded shelters for NRPF, but some non-governmental organisations (NGOs) and religious organisations provided shelters depending on geographical jurisdictions or experiences (drug use, sex work, domestic violence) (Homeless Link 2024). In addition, the Home Office made it illegal for landlords to rent to someone who does not have leave to remain or leave to enter. Landlords breaching these conditions could be fined up to £3,000 per adult or sentenced to up to five years in prison. These checks were deemed to breach human rights in 2019 due to their racialised effects (Hill and Taylor 2019) but the Home Office won an appeal in 2020 and the checks have been upheld (Gentleman 2020).

In Canada, precaritised residents can access emergency shelters in Toronto but not subsidised housing because it is provincially funded through the Social Housing Act and requires a UCI number (refugee number) and a SIN (social insurance number). Toronto Shelter Standards state that city-funded shelters may request information about a client's immigration status to assist them with obtaining or replacing identification and to determine their eligibility for social assistance programmes and related services. However, my interviewees reported that clients had been turned away from shelters due to their immigration status. Precaritised residents also left shelters because they feared the shelter service provider would report them to the CBSA.

For those who could not access shelters, lack of housing and gentrification were systemic problems in Toronto, forcing precaritised residents into dangerous dwelling situations. Interviewees reported that their undocumented clients found housing through support networks. Housing conditions were very poor, with overcrowding and the constant fear of being reported by landlords, co-dwellers or neighbours. Martina, a previously undocumented support worker described,

> Housing is so expensive and there is no access to social housing because it is provincially funded. So a bunch of people will rent an Airbnb. When there's no space left inside they will go to the patio and camp outside. But there is no contract. You have no tenant's right. So you can easily get evicted.

Service providers across all three cities stated that they no longer provided housing support because it is too time-consuming, and they were never successful. The dynamics that epitomise the neoliberalised city described in the Introduction pushed precaritised residents into dangerous housing conditions or out of the city entirely.

Health

In San Francisco, precaritised residents were eligible for Medi-Cal if they had a status called PRUCOL.[18] As Ceris, a policy analyst in the Human Services Agency described,

> We can give medical services for those considered PRUCOL. It generally means that we haven't found them in the database. But it's a very fuzzy category. There are many different types of PRUCOL but the most common one is that we take the statement on face value and can authorise someone for Medi-Cal without any further verification or documentation or checks on their identity and how they came to be in the U.S.

While this seemed to be standard practice, there was no clear understanding about whether ICE could use these checks to locate undocumented residents. Abigail, the deputy director of the HSA, conceded, 'there have been concerns that by checking with ICE we are indicating that someone is here. It's our understanding that it doesn't put our clients at risk'. She didn't provide any further details and it remains to be seen whether data sharing or interoperable databases will link health and immigration enforcement data.

For those that are not eligible for Medi-Cal, the HealthySF scheme was available to any resident in the city. Pablo, a health professional, explained that the record system sits entirely within the City Department of Public Health,

> We do ask for social security number but if you don't have it then we use 999-999-9999. The IT platform has no connection to Medi-Cal. And if we were to ever receive a subpoena for information from that electronic medical record from ICE or FBI our city attorney would file to prevent any disclosure of protected health information.

Community organisations explained that to access HealthySF in some cases they only needed to provide a cross street in San Francisco to meet eligibility requirements. However, not all services were free and many could not access them because of the cost.[19] Moreover, Marrow (2012) documents how HealthySF requires documentation that many precaritised residents cannot obtain and only includes primary care. While the city commits large resources to HealthySF and the programme morally sanctions precaritised residents as having a right to access healthcare, there are still many limitations to achieving equal access in practice.

In the UK, healthcare was based on a value that it was free at the point of access to all. However, since 23 October 2017, the government began charging tourists, overseas visitors, and precaritised residents in advance for healthcare, forcing hospitals and community health services to check every patient's documents, including passports and proof of address (Benchekroun and Humphris 2021). Non-urgent care was refused if a patient could not pay.

The National Health Service (NHS) began a data-sharing agreement with the Home Office in 2016 but, after a legal challenge, it withdrew from this agreement (Wemyss 2018). The NHS was sharing information with the Home Office if the patient had a hospital bill of more than £500 that had been unpaid for two months or more. The Home Office could also ask the NHS for the home address of a patient if they were trying to locate them. During 2020, the Home Office opened Covid-19 vaccination programmes for precaritised residents. However, as advocates stated, without concomitant assurances that they would not be traced and picked up for detention, precaritised residents would be too afraid to come forward (Benchekroun and Humphris 2021; Button et al. 2020a, b). There were fewer overseas visitor managers in wards questioning patients about their eligibility to healthcare during the Covid-19 pandemic; however, this meant more reliance on digital and remote means of charging.[20]

In Canada, the provinces decided eligibility for healthcare. There was no legislative requirement for a healthcare professional in Ontario to report a patient's immigration status to the CBSA (Martin 2020). However, individuals with precarious immigration status often found it difficult to access health-care services due to ineligibility.[21] Before March 2020, a person with no legal immigration status was ineligible for provincial health insurance. This meant that they were ineligible for both the Ontario Health Insurance Plan (OHIP) and the Interim Federal Health Program. They could therefore only access limited community services through the Community Health Centres (if they lived within their catchment area) and often bore the cost of their medical procedures.

Ontario had a three-month waiting period before any new resident to the province (with legal status or not) could gain OHIP. A network has developed for these uninsured residents and there was some leverage to push different levels of government on this issue because 'uninsured' could mean both those who do and do not have full legal migration status. Community Health Centres had provincial funding for 'uninsured' clients. This was used to cover all those that fell into this category, not only those who were categorised as 'three-month-wait'.[22]

Interviewees also described how hospitals had increasing budget deficits leading to stricter interpretations of regulations. While there were no reported incidents of CBSA conducting an immigration raid in a hospital, or anyone being reported to CBSA because they sought hospital care, similarly to San Francisco, the uninsured did not access care because of financial burdens.

In Toronto, access to healthcare outside immediate primary care depended on having an advocate or link with a network of support for precaritised res-idents. Access to primary care also depended on residential proximity to a

Community Health Centre. Midwives explained how they hired hotel rooms close to hospitals for uninsured clients to deliver babies to avoid medical fees, but if there was any problem, they could rush them to hospital quickly. Interviewees in San Francisco and Toronto also explained how physicians tried their best to ensure access, such as turning a blind eye when patients were clearly using someone else's health card.

Education

Public education was compulsory for all children across all three countries. The San Francisco Unified School District (SFUSD) set up a specific programme to assist newcomers and anyone who had legal status issues called 'Rise-SF'.[23] Maria, who ran the programme, delivered training on the sanctuary city laws and linked immigrant rights to anti-racist education for all trainee social workers in SFUSD. She explained her understanding of sanctuary,

> Sanctuary is about taking an active stance. We create spaces that are braver for our young people and for ourselves. We take a personal inventory around our own positionalities in the world and to check in with ourselves around our power and privilege in how we can support our young people and families. We try to impart that onto our staff so they can understand what sanctuary can be. We do a lot of work here at SF Unified around racial equity and our own implicit bias around our students and institutionalised white supremacy and the way that affects us as providers as teachers and educators and our young people. I try to bring it into our relationships with our students, the community at large and government and law enforcement.

San Francisco also voted for Proposition N, a charter amendment that extended the voting rights in San Francisco School Board election to non-citizen residents of San Francisco who were parents or legal guardians of children under the age of nineteen living in the city.[24] All residents of California could apply for in-state tuition for post-secondary education and there was limited financial aid available through the 2011 California Dream Act.

In the UK, all school-age children were required to go to school and no fees were required. As part of the school census, English schools were required by the Department for Education to collect the nationality and country of birth of children aged between five and nineteen. This information was not shared with the Home Office and it did not enter the National Pupil Database.

However, every month, the Home Office requested information collected through the school census to start re-investigating families who may be in the UK without leave to remain (Liberty 2019). The Home Office may ask the Department for Education to check the database for the addresses of specifically named people. Some schools asked to see children's passports although this was against government guidance (Hughes 2021). It was also reported that some schools only asked for the nationality and country of birth of visibly racialised children (Benchekroun and Humphris 2021).

In Toronto, access to education for the children of non-status and precarious status people was governed both by Ontario's Education Act[25] and by the Immigration and Refugee Protection Act.[26] The Education Act requires all school-age children in Ontario to attend school. The right to attend school in Ontario was therefore based on residence, not immigration status. However, the Education Act required school boards to charge tuition fees to certain students who were temporary residents (visitors specifically) in Canada or held study permits.[27] However, tuition fees were not charged to students if they or their parents were non-status, have made a refugee claim,[28] an application for permanent residence,[29] or an application for a work permit.[30] There was no legal requirement for education providers in Ontario to disclose the immigration status of their students, or their student's family, to the CBSA.

Even though non-status students were entitled to attend school, in practice, there were many reports that schools were wrongfully turning away many students because of their precarious immigration status. Interviewees also stated that rather than enrolling children at the school, parents were being told to enrol children at the Toronto District School Board headquarters in the outskirts of the city (see also Landolt and Goldring 2021; Villegas 2013, 2018). As Shimera, a sanctuary city advocate described,

> That's a really frightening step for a non-status family to have to take to get their kids into school. And I know I had one client last year they wouldn't let her child go to school and she was totally, like, legally entitled and legally required to go to school. And I had to go into the headquarters office and argue in order to get the kid into school.

These stories further indicate the wide gap between entitlements and enjoying rights in practice and the crucial role of gatekeepers in accessing all services.

Digital Welfare Bordering: Data Protection, Information Sharing,
and 'Firewalls'

In addition to the diffusion of immigration control into everyday life, residents can also be identified through data sharing and interoperable databases. Memoranda of Understanding between immigration enforcement (Home Office,[31] CBSA and ICE) and other government departments have been signed in each country.[32]

Developments in technology make the collection, retention, and linkage of large datasets much easier and increase the scale and speed at which data can be analysed and shared between different processors.[33] There is an increased emphasis on partnership working, data sharing, matching and mining in a range of policy areas.[34] The most efficient and well known was the Secure Communities programme which began in 2008 (rebranded as the Priority Enforcement Programme in November 2014). Fingerprints taken by local law enforcement were automatically run through the ICE database. If the person did not have a legal migration status, an immigration detainer was automatically issued and they would be placed in detention. Advocates in San Francisco developed several ordinances in response to Secure Communities to limit the information sharing between local and federal law enforcement (Humphris 2021). The focus in policy debates has been to construct firewalls between different parts of government and immigration enforcement. Employees in the Human Services Agency also raised the notion of 'one-way valves' where the municipal government can access data from federal databases but federal government cannot collect data from city services.

It is also important to note that immigration databases are often wrong either because they have made a mistake, someone's immigration status has changed and the system has not been updated, or they have erased information. An example of the latter is the Windrush scandal, where the UK Government conceded they had not kept proper records of people granted permission to stay in the UK (Narita 2023; Slaven 2021). The accuracy of one of these databases was challenged in the San Francisco district court. It was found to be so unreliable that it contravened the Fourth Amendment of the US Constitution on Due Process.[35]

Fear

This final section reviews three manifestations of fear as a bordering mechanism. The primary reason precaritised residents did not access their (limited) entitlements in sanctuary cities was fear of being reported. Even in San

Francisco, which has the most wide-ranging and visible sanctuary city policy, advocates and municipal officers alike were keen to point out that they could not stop anyone reporting someone as a private citizen even if they could forbid reporting as a municipal employee. In addition, as shown above, there were multiple ways that precaritised residents could be 'bureaucratically captured' by immigration enforcement across these three cities. As Silvia, a San Francisco children's family support worker described,

> We emphasise a lot that we are a sanctuary city. Many people don't know how it impacts them. They ask us 'how is that going to help me?' and so we explain that we are protected. But the reality is that even though we are a sanctuary city we still have ICE coming in. So there are a lot of conversations back and forth about that.

Fear in San Francisco reached new heights when Donald Trump's tenure as the 45th President of the United States began on 20 January 2017. As Carol, the manager of children's services in the Mission District described, 'sanctuary was always there but I don't think we used the terminology as much until we felt the impact of the election. We would get calls from families distraught saying, "I heard ICE is here in the Mission. I don't want to take my child to school. I don't want to leave my home"'. Linda, the head of a municipal service also reiterated, 'given the state of affairs nationally even those who want to take advantage of the sanctuary city are afraid to. The schools saw a decrease and some of the bus routes saw a decrease. People were afraid to go to work. We saw a decline in populations seeking assistance.'

Nazir, a key sanctuary activist in Toronto explained a similar situation: 'in many cases, even where services are available people won't go. . . . They cannot differentiate between a security guard, doctor, police or CBSA because that is collectively the government, which is why our campaign was about fear. And fear is not policy. Fear is about culture'. Despite the 'don't ask, don't tell' campaigns, many services in Toronto asked for migration status as a normalised process. Martina, a previously undocumented resident described, 'they need to stop asking people their status as the first question. I know for some shelters they ask, and they do not care what you write but for the person it is a big deal. They will just leave'. Similarly, in Sheffield, an employee of CoSS and a refugee, Fredrico, identified fear was exacerbated by services who constantly asked for migration status. 'It's not only the police or health service, they are checking on you everywhere. They check, "what is your status?" in every organisation. So there is fear everywhere. This is why some people fear even to take transport costs when they volunteer.'

In San Francisco, Silvia, a family support worker, described how they built trust with their clients to reduce fear, 'it's very important around how you are relaying the message, your vocabulary, your body language. You must create that space of trust with someone that you just met'. A crucial part of this messaging was not asking for more information than they needed, only asking once, and being very careful with that data. 'It's a very difficult balance between getting enough information to be able to provide services but also not holding data that we don't need or that would put people in danger. When we ask questions, we are starting with the why—why are we asking?' This practice of the service provider asking 'why' was reiterated across San Francisco service providers and was not evident in the other two cities.

The feeling of sanctuary to reduce fear was explained by Valentina, a support worker, as providing a 'circle of support'. She explains,

> For someone who comes here and has nobody and is completely isolated and you see it in their demeanour. They don't look at you much. They keep their head down. You feel it. You pick it up and you have to tell them—we are your community—we are your circle of support you can count on us.

This family resource centre also began hosting healing circles to help to reduce fear in response to the election of Donald Trump and the ICE raids that were taking place in surrounding counties. Amada, a support worker, explains,

> I was hearing about the attacks and the fear. I thought we need to provide some education of what protects us and we resorted to sanctuary. . . . There were a lot of healing circles that took place. To create space so anyone residing in the community could come and release and feel safe. There were lots of different types of sessions and holding space for people. It was very powerful. You could feel everyone's feelings. It was intense. It was a place to hold all of that and a place where people could talk through all of their fears and know that there was support here and regaining their power when they felt powerless.

In Toronto, similarly to the 'circles of support' mentioned above, Camilla, one previously undocumented resident, set up 'sanctuary suppers' to help inform precaritised residents about their rights. As the quote that opened this chapter explained, a central message she reiterated was that precaritised residents were residents, regardless of migration status. These suppers also provided practical support to reduce fear and exploitation,

> We are doing one about banking and how to get an ID. We tell people how to open a business and how to get a business number to be able to work. Companies are going to hire you only if you have a business number. They can say you were a subcontractor if there is any trouble. So many people need these business numbers so we are going to teach them how to get it because they are getting abused. There are agencies charging them around $800 to give them this number but it is actually $60 if they do it themselves. Those are the little things we are trying to do. We tell them you don't want to use your debit card because you don't want to leave any footprint. Buy a gift card. And I will teach them how to do it because I did it.

These networks of support that were evident across San Francisco and Toronto, indicate how sanctuary was used to assuage fear and build communities. A further sanctuary city practice was described as providing a 'warm transfer' between agencies in both Toronto and San Francisco. As Silvia, a family support worker, in San Francisco describes, 'if we are going to refer out to an agency then we have to be sure that they are going to follow the same principles as we do because families rely on us and trust us'. These practices have effects even though the sanctuary city provides no assurances against national immigration enforcement. Those who have previous experience of being undocumented and are embedded within communities are able to build relational practices that they place in terms of 'sanctuary'. In Sheffield, these practices may exist, but they were not placed under the name of the sanctuary city and therefore did not emerge in my fieldwork.

Final Remarks

This chapter has shown how bordering practices have shifted downwards to local scales, horizontally across institutions (which are not directly related to immigration), and across the public and private divide. Each city's hierarchies of enforcement shape whether residents are considered through the lens of their migration status or through their status as a resident of the city. This review indicates how these hierarchies are shaped by cities' legal constitutions, regulatory matrix, and policy context. In Sheffield, a wide range of people have specific duties to ask and report someone without a migration status with very harsh penalties for contravention, including prison sentences. These duties have reached beyond directly provided state services to private landlords and banks (Benchekroun and Humphris 2021). In Toronto, there was no duty to report, but no moral checks on people that did, and little training for frontline staff on the specificities of increasingly complex migration and settlement regulations. In San Francisco, there was a duty not to report accompanied by strong moral condemnation heavily backed up by 'the whole political tone of the city' (Lisa, director of a municipal service). Comparing these three sanctuary cities indicates that even with strong sanctuary city policies, the moral values that accompany them are just as important.

In addition, while laws and regulations establish the parameters for access, entitlements on paper are very different from practices on the ground. This chapter demonstrated the wide-ranging practices that emerge from sanctuary city policies. In San Francisco, organisations developed nuanced strategies to assuage precaritised residents' fears. If a resident did not give information such as a social security number, it was institutionalised practice 'not to push back' and to find a way to help. Ceris, a policy analyst for the Human Services Agency commented 'our instructions are to not push particularly hard on setting a high standard for what is a reasonable answer. So to the extent that there is some ambiguity we try to build practices where we treat all our clients equally'. This manifests in many ways. For example, this can include using a cross street as an address for HealthySF, or in child protection proceedings calling the embassy to do a background check rather than going through the FBI and fingerprinting family members.

In contrast in Toronto, a shadow network of service provision developed. Groups of individuals within organisations found bureaucratic openings to secure service for precarious status residents and had links across organisations, creating an informal and un-institutionalised welfare safety net. However, precarious status residents needed to find this network of support through serendipity or through their own networks. In Sheffield, there was no network (institutional or otherwise). Precaritised residents may have found isolated advocates who were willing and able to help them receive extremely limited support, but this was very sporadic and based on perceived need rather than entitlement. Across all cities, the effects of increasing digital infrastructure to circumvent these practices remains to be seen.

The following chapter will build on the legal and policy framework described here to explore the moral arguments that sanctuary actors used to account for themselves and what they are trying to do. This focus on morals is central to the workings of the sanctuary city. As mentioned above, even in San Francisco, municipal employees were aware they could not stop another employee reporting to ICE in a private personal capacity. As Nicole, an employee in the San Francisco District Attorney office described,

> What becomes hard as a city is that you can't prohibit an individual from communicating. So even if you set a policy that says you don't communicate it's a bit of a fallacy because you can't punish anybody for communicating. So what you're hoping is that you are leading with a moral vision that your city employees fall in line but if they don't, there is nothing you can do.

In the next chapter, I turn to examine the 'moral visions' or as I call them 'emergent moral values' of deservingness and membership that make up the sanctuary city.

FOUR

Negotiating Sanctuary
Emergent Moral Values

> I think we are pro-welcoming, rather than anti-racist. Sanctuary is about being
> a welcoming city. Being a positive City of Sanctuary that is proactive and com-
> mits to positive action, because it's the right thing to do, rather than defining
> yourself by what you're not, like anti-racism.
>
> Jane, Director of migrant-serving organisation, Sheffield.

This chapter traces the narratives of sanctuary actors and how they account
for themselves and what they are trying to do. These narratives are part of
an interactive process and could be animating or disarming by shifting notions of who belongs to the city, on what terms, and why. These narratives
also held ideas about how sanctuary actors defined the city and the nation,
understandings of their own positionality and how change might be achieved.
As the quote by Jane indicates, and will become clear below, sanctuary actors
defined their positions and beliefs very differently both between organisations and across different cities.

Recurrent common themes became evident through these narratives
which I have termed 'emergent moral values'. They are *emergent* because they
are always incomplete, in a constant state of becoming as they move through
different social contexts and actors and set in motion their own actions and
understandings. They are *moral* because they become the legitimate grounds
in terms of duties (mores) and principles (moralities) on which to include precaritised residents. They are *values* because they are sets of beliefs that are
relationally (re)produced, negotiated and contested between groups of actors.

This chapter lays out three emergent moral values that became evident in
the making of the sanctuary city. I term them, 'the efficient city', 'the healthy
city', and 'the just city'. All three circulated within each city and were not

mutually exclusive. These emergent moral values are perceived, embodied, and performed. As described in Chapter 1, emergent moral values of sanctuary act *on* and *through* the agency and subjectivity of actors.

The Efficient City

Narratives of the 'efficient city' coalesced around the idea that sanctuary city policy is good for the smooth running of the city. A well-functioning city is able to map, measure, and 'know' the city for the purposes of governing.[1] The efficient city is predictable, well organised, and minimises 'waste'. These characteristics also justify the city's legitimacy to govern. Mapping and measuring is key, allowing the city to plan the allocation of public services. The existence of residents that are not knowable and therefore not measurable represents a fundamental challenge to city governance. In addition, accurate measurement of the municipal population through the national census determines the amount of central government grant funds to provide services.[2] Undercounting exacerbates perceived scarcity. Cities negotiate the tension of making visible at the city level residents made invisible at the national level. However, city governments face two problems. First, residents are fearful of being counted because of the threat of deportation. Second, in a context of perceived scarcity, promoting services to precaritised residents is politically explosive. The following section traces how sanctuary city policy has provided an answer to these tensions through the emergent moral value of the 'efficient city'.

Labelling: Strategies and Unintended Consequences

The imperative to map and measure the population for the purpose of central grants led both San Francisco and Toronto to forbid employees to ask about migration status and both cities resolved not to collect migration status data, but with very different consequences. San Francisco created a government office with large grant making capacity for immigrant-focused programmes with the stated aim of building trust with communities. The office was originally set up to encourage those with precarious status to fill in the federal census. Anthea, the director of the office, explained in an interview in her office,

> In 2008, the Mayor was thinking about the upcoming census. The issue of paperwork doesn't matter because according to the Constitution we need to count everyone who is present in the United States. We started up as an office

at the end of 2008. We oversaw a citywide campaign for the census to make
sure people felt valued because we lose federal dollars. 25% of our population is
subject to not being counted.

Descriptions of the sanctuary city by bureaucrats often drew on this reading
of the US Constitution that does not mention legal citizenship. Precaritised
residents were not singled out but were folded into wider categories of people
who were not likely to fill in the census.

In contrast, Toronto created a new bureaucratic label 'Undocumented
Torontonians' in the 'Access T.O.' Ordinance in 2013, creating a distinct de-
finable population. The label raised precarious status residents' visibility but
set in motion a series of unintended consequences. First, the label formalised
precarious status residents allowing their inclusion in some bureaucratic
structures (for example, the Local Immigration Partnerships). However, as
federal government funds these structures, Undocumented Torontonians
were not a legitimate focus of concern and therefore did not gain benefits of
inclusion. Therefore, the label problematised and homogenised precarious
residents but with no concomitant resources to ameliorate marginalisation.
Gabriella, a frontline worker who worked in Scarborough, a 'downscaled'
area of Toronto, explained in the basement of a community centre where
she worked,

> By naming 'Undocumented Torontonians' they highlighted that there are
> people without status. It suddenly became an issue. Before that we served ev-
> eryone and we didn't even think about it.

Second, the introduction of Access T.O. curtailed some services in venues
that provided informal help to those without legal migration status. Gabriella has worked in the city for more than a decade. As we discussed her work
she went on to describe different stages of the programmes she's been part of
delivering,

> We did itinerant services in the library. They are city funded. And because my
> department would require eligibility, we were asking for Permanent Residency
> cards in the library. And we've been told, you cannot do that. You cannot ask
> for immigration documents while you are in the city facility. It's the same with
> schools. We cannot meet our targets if we keep serving those facilities, so we
> stopped the service.

Third, the condition that no city-level data could be kept on Undocu-mented Torontonians created further difficulties for service providers as men-tioned by Fiona, the director of a large and long-standing immigrant-serving organisation. I only managed to have a brief phone call with her because she was extremely busy and worked across Ontario. However, even as I quickly tried to get through as many questions as I could in the twenty minutes she had carved out to talk to me, she explained,

> We don't know how many people without legal immigration status are really accessing services. We only know anecdotally, for example, there are a number of folks who end up in shelters. But nobody has that data because we have the 'don't ask, don't tell policy'.

Finally, any conversation about 'Undocumented Torontonians' was care-fully curated by municipal officers. For example, 'Toronto for All' was a com-munity initiative that opened difficult city conversations. Previous topics included indigenous justice, anti-black racism, transgender youth of colour, and Islamophobia. However, Andrew, the director of municipal services, would not agree to a campaign for Undocumented Torontonians because of the risk of losing the policy. As he described, 'It was never solid. Right? It got through by stealth'. Therefore, there was concern about supporting a public awareness campaign to shape perceptions of 'Undocumented Torontonians'.[3]

The potentially politically explosive nature of Undocumented Toron-tonians coupled with the lack of data presented a problem for campaigners who wanted to expand the rights of non-status residents. Sanctuary actors turned to strategic labelling in one area of service provision: healthcare. In San Francisco, De Graauw details strategic labelling in the municipal ID card campaign (De Graauw 2014). Similarly, in Toronto, sanctuary actors used the category of 'medically uninsured'. This category included regular migrants who have not yet qualified for provincial healthcare insurance as well as those with no legal migration status. Framing 'Undocumented Torontonians' as 'medically uninsured' explains the strategic silence of campaigners about expanding healthcare rights to precaritised residents (Humphris 2020). In contrast, Sheffield has made no such commitment and precaritised residents are only discussed in terms of asylum seekers and refugees, or asylum seekers who have exhausted appeal rights and become 'No Recourse to Public Funds'. There is no recognition of any other form of precaritised resident within discussions of the City of Sanctuary (such as falling out of work, study, spousal visa requirements).

To summarise, in Toronto, labelling residents with diverse migration statuses and experiences in one bounded category created a single and homogenising abstraction to be governed, raising visibility and setting in motion unpredictable bureaucratic and political processes. Limited advances were made by engaging in strategic labelling in one area of service provision. In contrast, in San Francisco, strategic silence and broad labelling from the outset extended legitimate treatment for precaritised residents. In Sheffield, there was no recognition and no concomitant policy.

Both Toronto and San Francisco have made a commitment that they will not ask about migration status. This commitment places a particular set of requirements on the frontline because eligibility for state or provincial and federal government funded programmes is contingent on legal migration status. The city administration therefore relies on frontline workers to know but not document migration status. The city makes this strategic move, to 'unsee' at one moment (and diffusing the responsibility to the frontline to know the people using their service and to use funding in sometimes unauthorised ways) so that they can 'see' more clearly at another (for example building trust so that residents complete the national census).

Frontline Work in the 'Efficient' Sanctuary City

In San Francisco, extending City programmes to precaritised residents was narrated in terms of efficiencies. Efficiency included frontline workers' time and energy. Near the beginning of my fieldwork, I interviewed Ceris, a policy analyst in the San Francisco HSA in a large, labyrinthine building in the east of the city where many of the bureaucratic headquarters were based. She explained,

> Sanctuary is an efficiency in terms of our federal programs because sometimes it is not easy to identify where the line is around authorised immigrant or unauthorised immigrant and attempting to work out eligibility based along those lines.

Linda, a San Francisco probation officer, indicated another meaning of efficiency, 'it is just one thing we don't have to worry about—we don't have to identify them or serve them any differently. The flow of services is the same so that makes it more efficient. There is no different tracking system. There is no different reporting procedure. Everyone is treated the same and fairly'. Efficiency is put to work to make the process 'fair' if not 'equal' at least in value terms. This has resonance with the value of citizenship of treating everyone fairly and equally before the law regardless of their background. As a value it functioned for certain purposes, while in practice it did not work in such a way.

Sanctuary policies could extend the reach of bureaucratic processes and fold potentially unlikely agents into becoming a 'face of the state' (Humphris 2018). Support workers in San Francisco were painfully aware of this aspect of their role and described how they tried to build trust with residents and determine their eligibility for services without asking for migration status. Liliana, a San Francisco community support worker, explained while we drank sweet Vietnamese coffee in the predominantly Latinx Mission District,

> The City has been very flexible on the documents they accept for verification of income, identity and address. The current form doesn't need the community member to sign it. They don't need to give us their address. We can use cross streets, so we just know what area they are living in and what neighbourhoods are being served. The City has worked with us in that way to make it accessible but only because we pushed for it. We had a strong advocacy plan and we have been able to push for those things.

These advocacy efforts also helped to release frontline workers from moral dilemmas that emerged in their work, particularly around mandated reporting (Furman et al. 2012, 176). As Juliet, the director of a nationwide NGO for elderly services, explained,

> We've had issues when we've needed to call in Adult Protective Services. In one instance, an adult child told our social worker that her father with dementia was being financially abused by his landlord. Because of his illegal status, he wasn't able to call the police for help. We are legally bound to report instances of elder abuse regardless of immigration status and found ourselves having to inform authorities—in order to protect him. This was in San Mateo County. It definitely felt like a no-win situation. We don't have situations like that for our clients in San Francisco.

Crucially, directors of municipal departments, vendors of city services, and non-profits identified the current economic position of San Francisco as a defining factor in the attitude of the City to be flexible in terms of eligibility for city-funded services. As we sat in her large office around a conference table that was full of papers, leaflets, and folders, Abigail, the deputy director of San Francisco's HSA, stated,

> County context makes a difference here—we are a very liberal city and we also have more resources. We have access to city funds and county funds. We have had an unprecedented amount of economic growth as a city, as a county, as a state. We haven't had to face questions around resources and whether we fund citizens over immigrants. Under Governor Brown we were in huge debt and deficits in California. Those questions come up a lot more in those contexts even in places that have liberal values. We don't have to make those opportunity costs.

The wealth of the city afforded a particular interpretation of sanctuary as efficient in San Francisco. For example, Ling, director of a Chinatown community organisation, reiterated that city affluence meant they would be able to continue their programmes for all residents (including all precaritised residents),

> Even though my hands are not directly in the sanctuary world it provides the City with an attitude that I get to work within. Without it, the work with undocumented would become a personal decision as a CEO. You would have to get sign-off from the board. In SF, we don't have to waste our energy with that. Compliance is a big deal—you would have to make the decision, are we going to give up a million dollars and not have the funds to do the work? We have the benefit of being sanctuary but also being the hub of so much wealth. It's a massive benefit.

Ling's quote identifies the issue that directors of immigrant-serving organisations faced in Toronto. Due to the legal constitution of the city, access to services and city funds was extremely limited. However, by acknowledging 'Undocumented Torontonians' the city devolved the decision about whether to serve this group to individual CEO's of NGOs. Returning to Fiona on our rushed phone call she explained,

> It is about the leadership of NGOs. There is downloading in terms of service access from the City to NGOs. The funding regime lends itself to that. The largest funder of services is the federal government and they are very clear and restrictive in terms of eligibility.

In Toronto, a complex shadow system of services emerged precisely because of the diffusion of responsibility from the City to NGOs. Frontline workers encountered dilemmas where their professional values conflicted with eligibility requirements. A large amount of work was unaccounted, unaccountable, and unfundable. Frontline workers supported precaritised residents voluntarily. Alexia, a manager of a community organisation in the centre of Toronto, described to me as we discussed her work in a Chinese restaurant in the Kensington Market area of Toronto, 'it really depends on the motivation of the leaders of that program. A person who runs a settlement program can make a decision on the spot. It's all down to whether you have a culture of support'. Bianca, a support worker in a women's organisation, described a similar situation, 'we have two different databases, we have the government database, and then we have our own internal database. We don't keep as much data on the undocumented because we do not ask beyond what we need, and we are not funded for that work.'

Moreover, frontline workers reiterated working with precaritised residents was difficult, emotional, and complex work and only those who 'have a heart' for it can build the relationships needed. Shamira, an executive director of a community organisation, introduced me to Martina, a support worker who was previously undocumented. We sat together in a small windowless office that Martina used for consultations with clients. It was empty apart from a desk with a telephone and four chairs that only just fit in the room. Martina explained,

> I know the organisations that judge if they don't have status. I was a person without status for six years. I understand their struggle and why they are afraid. . . . I love this job. Any small thing I do in my job is an achievement—to see some other people happy. I'm dying for this.

Executive directors explained the difficulty in finding staff that could serve non-status people particularly because they could not publicly hire staff to take on these roles. Shamira detailed this when Martina had to leave the room because she had an emergency phone call from one of her clients who was being evicted,

> There is no formal on-boarding process or training process for people to work with undocumented because it's not a part of our funding. It's not something

we do. But the reality is we do see a lot of people and we do have to recognize that we need to provide services for them. But it's never really talked about. You could lose your funding.

Salim, the executive director of a neighbourhood organisation, explained that his staff see precaritised residents outside their work hours, 'we are doing a lot of extra services that's not being accounted and we're happy to do that. Our staff stay half an hour late, come half an hour early and do those kind of things. They feel proud of doing that. We don't have any employee who's not willing to do that'. It has been well-established in neoliberal governance that there is a growing disparity between bureaucratic reporting and actual practice (Humphris 2019). Rather than creating 'sceptical subjects' and 'petri dishes for discontent' (Clarke and Newman 1997), Salim described how individualised subjects take pride in this unaccounted extra work as it forms part of their identity as a service provider and caring subject (see also Shore et al. 2011, 21). Those who are able to build trusting relationships with precaritised residents often share a language or may be co-nationals such as Martina mentioned above, raising issues linked to advanced marginalisation (Cohen 1999). In Toronto, the 'efficient sanctuary city' had the consequence of creating a shadow system of services and devolved responsibility to marginalised residents to govern those more marginalised.

The 'efficient city' moral value was mobilised differently in Sheffield. In a unitary government and context of a hostile environment coupled with austerity-localism, municipal officers used 'efficiency' to justify reporting undocumented residents to the Home Office. Austerity-localism fuelled a sense of risk and refusal with financial efficiency and cost-saving at its core. Both precarious and non-precarious status migrant residents found it difficult to access city services. Henry, a municipal employee whose role was to support recognised refugees' access to services, explained in an interview in the City of Sanctuary offices. I met him at half past six in the evening when everyone else had left the office, but he was still doing paperwork and getting calls from clients with requests for help. In a hushed voice, even though the office was empty he recalled,

I've gone to the Job Centre, and they will not let them in. Even at the Council where I am an employee, if I am not there, they will send them away. My own colleagues. That's the fact.

Rather than a dilemma between professional code of practice and eligibility criteria, bureaucrats reframed their professional duties to include reporting in the name of efficiency. I interviewed two members of the children's services team, Frances and Jacqueline, in a meeting room in their office. Frances explained,

> For me, it feels really clear cut. . . . Everyone is always reported to the Home Office. It's untenable otherwise, isn't it? Unless you kick in to reporting there's no progress in any way, shape or form. People are just kept waiting. Things will never be resolved.

Financial efficiency is leveraged within these discussions as a standardised process which is depoliticised through the language of efficiency and practicality. Jacqueline, also in the children's services team, explained,

> There is no never ending pot of money. We have to be realistic with that. If we could get a family to return, then that would be absolutely fine. We will pay the flight upfront because actually, that for us is cheaper in the long run. We would always offer that as a first instance.

Moreover, the police and the Home Office openly collaborated, primarily justified by 'efficiency'. There was no countervailing argument, for example, the sanctuary narrative in San Francisco Police Department that this kind of police cooperation would undermine the purpose of police to serve the community, which relied on building relations of trust.

Summing up the efficient city

The 'efficient city' is an emergent moral value where sanctuary is mobilised to balance different aims. This moral value is underpinned by the will to govern, to map and measure the population to fulfil governing duties. As a corollary to measurement, within neoliberal governance rationalising local government action is focused on minimising 'wasted' resources. However, in each city 'efficiency' and what constitutes 'waste' is defined differently. For example, in San Francisco, 25 per cent of the population had precarious status and were afraid to complete the national census. 'Unseeing' undocumented residents in the detail of service provision allows more accurate accounting in the census, which determines federal grants to the municipality. However, sanctuary actors did not solely frame efficiency as financial resources. The police included community trust in their understanding of 'efficiency'. The HSA defined efficiency as frontline workers' time and removing moral dilemmas.

In Toronto, with a city-level policy, but no city-level funding, unintended and paradoxical consequences of Access T.O. abounded, as decisions regarding inclusion were diffused to the Executive Directors or individuals working in frontline services. Some organisations refused to serve undocumented clients. Others developed systems of shadow provision and reporting that bore scant resemblance to frontline workers' daily practice. This reveals a clear contradiction within efficiency: that it relies on unseen, unaccountable work by those employed in the lowest levels of bureaucracy (increasingly on short-term, precarious contracts who may themselves be subjected to border controls). In contrast, in the UK's unitary system, Sheffield's sanctuary actors had very little room for manoeuvre due to bureaucratic structures and their concomitant funding regimes. Coupled with austerity-localism and the hostile environment, frontline workers' primary goal was to reduce spending. In this context, efficiency was defined as cooperation with the Home Office due to a culture of bureaucratic risk and refusal of services, and rising nativism.

The Healthy City

The second moral value that justified sanctuary city policies emerged around arguments that inclusion promotes a safe and healthy city. As shown below, sanctuary actors mobilised these narratives to argue that sanctuary policies were 'best for everyone' because of public health and public safety. In San Francisco, healthy city arguments were at the forefront of how sanctuary actors mobilised others. Abigail, deputy director of San Francisco's HSA, stated, 'there is the health argument that you don't want undocumented people to spread diseases because they can't access the hospital as well as from the lens of public safety'. Anthony, a director of a criminal justice department, reiterated and expanded on the notion,

> Somebody needs healthcare, they have measles, they have some other health situation that could be a public health situation. It's important they have confidence and be allowed to access healthcare because it could impact all of us. I think from a bigger picture perspective, that's where our policies are important because they lead to a healthier city—when I say healthy I mean in terms of public safety, public health, public education.

In Toronto, references were made to a generalised 'public opinion' that acknowledged the existence of precaritised residents as a problem that the city should act upon for the health and growth of the city. However, a different set of arguments based on labour market participation and demographics are entwined with framing precarious status residents as potential vectors for disease or perpetrators of crime. Nick, a Toronto city councillor, clearly articulated this merging of health of residents with the health of the city's economy,

> What good is it to us as a city to marginalize and make invisible and push these people underground. They're going to have higher disease rates, higher crime rates, because people are going to do what they need to do to eat and to live. . . . And rich countries know that bottom line. You want to deal with those folks in a coherent, consistent, holistic manner? And take them out? Your economy falls apart.

Nick clearly articulates the fundamental tension sanctuary is aimed to solve between wealth creation (flexible low-wage labour) and promoting a just distribution of resources. Karen, the director of an immigrant-serving organisation, also reiterated this perspective, 'We're keeping Canada alive. We need people to come here to have babies because white people are not having many babies to run the country. It's our future. Refugees. Immigrants. That is the future of Canada. That's what's going to keep our country healthy and growing'. Population management was therefore a salient issue in Toronto's 'healthy city' emergent moral value that held weight when trying to mobilise others under the sanctuary city policy.

The narrative that migrants' health has consequences for the wellbeing of the city and the nation was also evident in Sheffield but was inflected through the prism of austerity-localism and cost-savings. The dominant narrative in Sheffield was based on the principle of welcome and hospitality as Michele, a community development officer, explained, 'we have never had to use the public health kind of argument. It's about the welcomeness and the friendliness of the city'. However, while the idea of being a welcoming city was at the forefront of public narratives, in practice, the public health department funded the asylum seeker drop-in. As Dave, the co-chair of an integration advisory group, explained over a cup of tea at his house near the centre of Sheffield,

> Previously the Council had been the coordinator of the asylum seeker drop-in but they had to pull out. City of Sanctuary agreed to step into that role. And the director of public health was an ally at the time, and he had a bit of money in his budget and he agreed to put it in. The argument was the risk of communicable diseases. There are all these people in the city, and they won't have access to health care. If we have the drop-in we know where they are and we can support them but it was also like a monitoring aspect.

Discourses of risk, scarcity and investing in the present to guard against increased costs in the future pervaded descriptions of the sanctuary city within Sheffield. In contrast to Toronto where precaritised residents were included to secure the city's future health, in Sheffield, precaritised residents were included because of the risk of future cost. This argument has its roots in the 'social investment state' (Dobrowolsky and Lister 2008) but has been reworked through austerity and retrenchment. The future now holds financial risks requiring mitigation in the present. Jackie, a director of municipal services, explained the current situation at the frontline while identifying what she believed would be a better practice,

> They [frontline gatekeepers] get it wrong. They would prefer not to take the risk. And actually we should do the right thing. If you've got TB, or measles. But that doesn't seem to have much purchase because we are so strapped for cash. And they cannot see the people that they have already. And they need to recoup those funds. . . . When I say 'do the right thing' what I mean is to risk seeing the people, right, and don't be risk averse, not thinking, I ain't gonna get the money back from seeing this. . . . It's empowering people on the frontline to take the risk and care for people. We'll take the financial risk as well, because actually, it might cost us less in the long run, because then we might have multiple cases of TB.

Here the notion of the healthy and safe city was based on a value of investment, that resources should be spent in the present to guard against increased cost in an imagined future, indicating the pervasiveness of austerity-localism. However, as Jackie describes, frontline workers do not even take this risk because of the cost.

The Healthy City: Best for Everyone?
The limitations of leveraging 'healthy city' narratives were well acknowledged by some sanctuary actors. Three main arguments against these narratives

were evident. First, from the position of elected officials, sanctuary protects legal citizens, not all residents, as Vijay, a municipal employee working in a department responsible for human rights in San Francisco, described, 'it's designed to make documented people feel concerned for undocumented people because it's best for them (documented) and it's about their own safety. That's how you build buy in'. While the healthy city moral value was the most effective at building consensus for including precaritised residents in city services it also limited the potential to think differently about inclusion and belonging in the city.

Second, this moral value reinforced the pejorative link between migration and criminalisation. As Hannah, a San Francisco human rights lawyer, explained,

> ICE has increasingly sold itself as a public safety agency not an immigration agency—it's not about whether your papers are in order, it's about saving you from criminals. We know police target black, brown and immigrant communities. Police treat these people as guilty until proven innocent and so does ICE. It's all part of the same dynamics. But that's why it's difficult for us to keep them separate because it's claiming that anyone who looks like this is a threat.

Notions of public safety, while seemingly inclusive, reinforce the criminalisation of migration and (re)produce fears.

Third, and finally, sanctuary actors in grassroots community-led organisations were quick to point out that sanctuary policies do not create safer or healthier communities because precaritised residents remain afraid of the police. Like the 'efficient city', the 'healthy city' fails to acknowledge and unsettle hegemonic understandings of belonging. The healthy city leads to an understanding of precaritised residents as a potential underclass that threatens the health and safety of the city.

Summing up the healthy city

This moral value draws on the fear of creating an 'underclass' to mobilise practices towards precaritised residents but emerges and is defined in different ways in each city. The underlying similarity is an imagined future that draws on fears of a potential dystopian city with a growing, uneducated, lawless population that is rife with disease and a hotbed of crime and disorder. Fear is always constituted in relation to others who are feared and therefore is social and relational. Since the inception of cities, there have always been conceptions of others who represent disorder and danger such as paupers, vagrants, and degenerates (Rose 1999) and these figures have been reconfigured to include working classes, immigrants, LGBTQI+, youth, and others. This fear 'touches our rawest nerves and often calls upon some of our most visceral responses: to defend our own, not to surrender, to patrol our borders, to suspect the stranger; to exclude, reject and shun (Sparks et al. 2001, 885). Those who draw on these narratives aim to unsettle pejorative or exclusionary sentiments; however, those who mobilised the healthy city moral value at their best reproduced contingent belonging and at their worst affirmed the space of the city as a place of disorder and disease, positioning the precaritised resident as the figurehead. Precaritised residents' presence is 'tolerated' contingent on constantly shifting notions of deservingness.

The Just City
The third emergent moral value of sanctuary was based on notions relating to ideas of 'justice'. I do not define justice here, but rather present the different narratives that held an idea of sanctuary as the right (mores) and good (morality) thing to do. Many different words operated in semantic clusters with 'sanctuary' such as fairness, being good, being ethical, upholding a moral code, social justice, economic justice, equality, and contribution. What is seen as 'fair' and who is seen as 'deserving' involves symbolic struggles and a way of determining those individuals who do not 'belong' along multiple dimensions. I have organised this section to move from those that represented the most widely held understandings to the smaller numbers of sanctuary actors who raised limitations and objections to these more commonly held understandings of 'justice' and were practising alternative notions.

Contribution
The most pervasive manifestation of a 'just' moral value rested on notions of contribution. The idea that precaritised residents contributed to the city sought to engage residents' feelings of a reciprocal relationship that had been formed between them and precaritised residents of the city. Bonds were created through social, economic, and political relations. However, these relations also created duties and obligations, which could shift at any moment,

invoking ideas of continual probationary citizenship. This notion of contribution was also entrenched in 'presentism', not accounting for histories of negative reciprocal relations (see Chapter 2).

Contribution was evident in all three cities but understood differently. It was effective at building public consensus because it meant many different things to different people and it shifted its meaning while holding coherence and intelligibility across different contexts. The nature of contribution also resonated with fundamental understandings of reciprocity and debt. Cyrus, a San Francisco Supervisor, clearly laid out his perception of the sanctuary city along these lines,

> We have a cross section of the population that contributes immensely to the economy, contributes immensely to the fabric of the city but yet they don't have the same rights. To me that is problematic. . . . Just like everybody else, our undocumented population works hard, they want the best for their children, they contribute to our economy. You can't take people's resources, take their labour, and then turn around and say we don't want them to have the same rights.

The argument based on contribution led to advances in the political rights of precarious status migrants in San Francisco. For example, undocumented residents can vote in School Board elections and serve on City and County Committees. Sanctuary actors in that campaign used the same arguments based on notions of contribution. Here contribution was not just economic, but also about being part of the political and social fabric of the city.

Contribution was also mobilised in Toronto to extend acceptance of precaritised residents; however, contribution was solely framed in economic terms. Karen, a city vendor[4] of refugee services, explained,

> All these people are contributing. People working under the table are contributing. They are in the construction industry. They're shopping in grocery stores and keeping the economy going. You know, whether you're a refugee claimant, a migrant, a worker under the table. Everybody's contributing to the economy of this country to survive. And everybody has a right to survive. To have a better life.

In Sheffield, the notion of contribution was not explicitly discussed but was implicitly evident through the support that was given to asylum seekers who volunteered at migrant support organisations. Those who volunteered were seen to be 'doing the right thing' and were supported.[5] Fredrico, a previous refugee who worked at a support organisation, described the conditional nature of contribution, 'even with work experience, you can tell that there is a limit. There is a bar drawn. Like, this job is not for you. However beautifully you might contribute, you are not like us. That is the feeling'. Despite different contexts and notions of 'contribution', sanctuary actors recognised the same limitations of this argument for sanctuary. Contribution, while effective at building public consensus for inclusion of precaritised residents, is based on the idea of a 'model minority' (Lee 2015). These residents are only tolerated as long as they fit into a proscribed role which is probationary, contingent, and shifting (Anderson 2013).

These limits of contribution-based arguments emerged in different ways in each city. In San Francisco, precaritised residents charged with crimes placed the limit of contribution-based arguments into stark relief as articulated by Anthony, a city vendor for criminal justice,

> Is a DUI [driving under the influence] enough to deport someone? Is there a rubric for what triggers an ICE thing? Is there a rubric for what your contribution to this country is? If this has been your home for life, then it's a different question compared to whether you came here three months ago and are causing havoc and going on a crime spree? I know there are human rights like your right to live in a free society but if you're breaking the social contract in every way, should you be protected? One factor is the length of time you've been here, what was your route, do you have a family?.

Anthony's questions exemplify the axiomatic assumptions underpinning this moral value. Precaritised residents are not considered equal to another resident charged with a crime who would be dealt with solely by the criminal justice system. As Joanne, a human rights lawyer, explained,

> The criminal justice system doesn't solve our issues but adding immigration to it doesn't solve our issues either. If you are worried about murder or rape— deporting someone is not going to help these issues or solve them. That is an incorrect analysis. Even with very progressive elected officials, they say—well if someone does something very bad, I think they shouldn't be here. And then we ask, what if someone wasn't an immigrant and they are charged with murder— how do you solve that? How do we really solve violent crime in our city? We try to have that conversation.

The entwining of immigration and criminalisation provoked seemingly unanswerable debates about where to draw the line of 'deservingness'. Contribution provides a partial answer and creates a moral standpoint based on length of residence, adherence to the 'social contract', the severity of the crime, and adherence to a heteronormative value of the 'family'. These conditions are narrated as post-hoc justifications through which precaritised residents can be excluded, effectively hiding the contingent belonging and unequal treatment underpinning this value when mobilised for the sanctuary city.

In Toronto, arguments based on contribution were mobilised by anti-migrant campaigners to craft their own targeted narratives. These narratives were aimed at recently arrived Torontonians. They sought to turn these Torontonians against precaritised residents by claiming precaritised residents 'jumped the queue' and had therefore cheated their way into Canada. This narrative held a lot of weight in popular narratives in Toronto, particularly in the wake of irregular arrivals crossing the border from the United States following Donald Trump's 'Muslim Ban' policy.

Narratives of scarcity also revealed the limits of contribution and how it could be used to undermine equality. Resource constraints, particularly in Toronto and Sheffield, revealed the underlying hierarchy in these arguments. In Toronto, scarcity most starkly emerged in discussions around healthcare provision where there was a perception that only taxpayers should receive healthcare because they pay for it. I met Kathlyn, public health employee, at a Network for Uninsured meeting and she agreed to meet me for a coffee afterwards to discuss her experiences of Toronto's sanctuary city. As we sat in a shopping mall coffee shop, she explained, 'if you're working under the table, even if you're paying taxes, because you're not documented, you're not seen as legitimate for access'. Here, we can see the limits of the contributing argument. Paying taxes does not move a precaritised resident into the realm of legitimacy; services must be reserved for 'legitimate taxpayers'. This indicates the underlying contradictions within the idea of contribution, and how it is mobilised as a mode of exclusion rationalised through 'just' distribution of resources.

Humanitarianism

In all three cities, personalised stories were used by advocates that connected individuals with different forms of legitimacy through victimhood. These included workplace injury, gender-based violence or life-threatening health conditions. These strategies did not unsettle dominant narratives of deserv-ingness because they were portrayed as 'exceptional' cases. However, they did provide constrained avenues for individuals to claim rights (cf. Fassin 2011). Narratives that centred on the female suffering body were particularly effective to gain exceptional rights. Swati, a Toronto human rights lawyer, explained, 'I hate to say it but when you present those really tragic women's stories, those are the ones that catch the eye of politicians'. She described how she placed herself outside these arguments, but mobilised them when they served a function for a client because victimhood opened a small foothold for rights.

Pallister-Wilkins defines humanitarianism as 'logics developed for the maintenance of liberal order alongside and through the securing of life' (2020, 991), but where some are deemed more deserving of support than others (Armbruster 2019; Holmes and Castañeda 2016). In Sheffield and Toronto, the treatment of Syrian refugees is a case in point. Returning to Kathlyn,

> With the Syrian refugees there is this idea of compassion being extended. You see people feeling like they are in abundance, and not in scarcity. That doesn't extend to undocumented people.

Humanitarianism has been conceived as 'depoliticizing' (Ticktin 2014) as emotional responses such as compassion replace a broader quest for rights (Fassin 2011; Danewid 2017). A distinction is often made in scholarship be-tween humanitarian action and political action with humanitarianism placed 'outside' and neutral to politics. Humanitarian compassion can extend and counter the limitations inherent in scarcity narratives but are also strongly contingent and set in motion their own criteria for 'inclusion'. In Sheffield, this distinction was reproduced through the narratives of the volunteers who set up the first emergency shelters and cash support for destitute asylum seekers in 2002 (see Humphris 2020). A volunteer engaged with this work at the time commented, 'I think the motivation was what I would probably call humanitarian. I think it wasn't strongly political'. Similarly, the quote that opened this chapter from Jane, the director of a migrant-serving organisa-tion in Sheffield, reiterated this understanding of political by framing their work outside 'politics', placing it rather in moral terms about the 'right' thing to do. Jane had a background in media and communication and was focused on providing positive stories about asylum seekers in the face of stereotypes and scapegoating. However, this perspective also effectively sidestepped any discussion about the wider structural inequalities faced by racialised and minoritised residents that might place obligations and duties on these service providers. Rather, this perspective continues to place service providers in the realm of 'helping' and sees asylum seekers solely as recipients of care granted through the generosity and compassion of volunteers rather than a sense of solidarity or duty.

In Sheffield, the notion of hospitality, welcome, and compassion, while in some circumstances could unsettle logics of scarcity through strong affective responses particularly to mediatised images of suffering (see Humphris and Yarris 2022), is also predicated on an idea of generosity that can equally find its limitations through rationing of emotional and financial resources. This is evident both in city-level government (making opportunity costs such as not completing human rights assessments) and within third sector and voluntary organisations. Many immigrant-serving organisations in Sheffield relied on private donations and volunteers who had a particular conception of the types of people they should be 'helping'. Fredrico, a previous CoSS worker and refugee, explained, 'so it is like they have this general belief of lowness. There's that feeling that a refugee is supposed to be someone who is poor. Someone who is not supposed to be able to provide. Someone who should not have any voice'. The focus on sanctuary as humanitarian, as the right thing to do to help the needy, rather than as an obligation or duty hid the power imbalances and the pervasiveness of guest-host relations.

In San Francisco, there was no explicit discourse around hospitality or 'welcome' linked to the sanctuary city. Welcome was perceived as something very different from the sanctuary city. Indeed the 'Welcoming America' initiative can be conceived as a case of 'policy mobility' from the UK City of Sanctuary movement to the USA through a policy network. Welcoming was incongruent to many in San Francisco who had been living in the city for decades or had family living in the city for generations.

Fairness

Notions of fairness were mobilised in sanctuary actors' narratives in Toronto and San Francisco but were absent from how the sanctuary city was discussed in Sheffield. In San Francisco, 'fairness' was linked to constitutional rights of 'due process'. Hazel, a children's rights lawyer, who had been involved in the early social movement for the sanctuary city through the 'Due Process for Youth' Ordinance, explained how undocumented residents' treatment shook the foundations of legitimate governance centring her families' lived experience,

> One of the things that was most upsetting to me was the fundamental unfairness. Two kids could go and smoke pot in the park and for one it would have barely any consequences and for the other it would be tragic. It completely undermines those teenagers' faith in institutions. . . . It's to do with the social fabric and when that breaks down, it all breaks down.

The idea of fairness that emerges in this description mixes notions of social justice, equitable treatment, faith and trust in institutions, public safety, integrity, upholding the 'social fabric' or 'social contract', and the legitimacy of governing. Unlike the description of the moral dilemmas by the criminal justice employee based on 'contribution' above, Hazel does not adhere to the 'common sense' view that immigration and criminal justice are entwined, or that because someone is a migrant that fact overrides any other discussion on what is fair treatment. When this link between immigration and criminalisation is broken, new and unsettling questions emerge regarding the fundamental principles on which society is organised and the legitimacy of the laws and institutions on which society is based. She also links this to her role as a parent and the need to be able to explain to her own children the nature of authority they perceive as unjust. This does not concern an idea of trust to co-opt residents into governing programmes, but rather if institutions treat undocumented residents unfairly, documented residents will stop believing in those institutions and the social fabric will rupture. Here a further aspect of living together in the city is revealed, undocumented residents live together with citizens, breaking down the 'us and them' divide through the practices of living and making families together. When this divide is unsettled the institutional legitimacy of governing is questioned.

The meaning of fairness that emerges when precaritised residents are seen as co-urban dwellers rather than national guest-host relations was also reiterated by Swati who was at the forefront of sanctuary organising in Toronto,

> I think, like what we were trying to do was make our politicians understand who we're talking about, right? Because they talk in these very nebulous terms, and they don't know who undocumented people are. It's the woman living

in the basement apartment next door to you with two kids. We're trying to make people understand that these are your neighbours, the people in your community.

As residents become entwined, exceptional practices towards precaritised residents become judged as illegitimate, raising questions about the legitimacy of governance itself. For some who took this perspective, the answer to these questions was to operate outside the law.

Breaking Rules

Sanctuary actors who perceived extant governing frameworks as unjust crafted different narratives that were not based on balancing conflicting governing logics, or pragmatically leveraging arguments in the service of incremental 'progressive' change. In both San Francisco and Sheffield, sanctuary actors drew on histories of previous city activism to describe how they were operating outside the current governing framework. Valentina, a sanctuary actor in San Francisco's Mission District, explained, 'the sanctuary of the 80s is good to draw from. They acted because the laws were messed up. They were broken. We need to go outside the system to protect the rights of people because the laws aren't protecting the rights of people'. This quote indicates a reimagining of the 1980s sanctuary context. The sanctuary movement in the 1980s did not aim to operate outside the law, but rather aimed to uphold the laws they perceived the US government were violating (by not granting refugee status to those fleeing war in Central America). In Valentina's narrative she gains inspiration and mobilises a reworking of the history of sanctuary entwining contemporary notions of abolitionism[6] with an acknowledgement that this is not a defined or visible path but is emerging through their practice.

A similar notion was narrated by Matt, one of the founding members of ASSIST, a charity set up in Sheffield in response to the dispersal of asylum seekers in 2002,

> You often have a barometer of what's acceptable by what your legal framework is. But the legal framework was wrong. So the legal framework is not a barometer through which you can check whether your activity is acceptable or not. I think there were a lot of legitimate questions that we didn't even think of asking because we thought why would you check what the law says because the law is wrong.

He reflects an uncertainty about operating without a socially sanctioned guide to their activities and finding their own sense of what is 'just'. In this absence, similarly to sanctuary actors in San Francisco, he turned to the radical history of Sheffield as a form of narrating actions into a longer memory of resistance in the city. A similar history was mobilised by Ingrid, a human rights lawyer in Sheffield,

> In Sheffield there is a history of when the law is wrong we'll make it right. And I think trespass is a great example of that—the law is wrong and we will take action until it's right. The miners' strike is a big part of Sheffield and I can remember being in school and going to soup kitchens because of the miners' strike. Government is wrong so we'll take action until the Government sees that we're right. And we will keep on doing that.

In Toronto, understanding why people break the rules was informed by personal migration experiences. As Nick explained as I sat in his kitchen eating eggs laid by the urban chickens in his garden,

> We don't pin down capital but we pin down people. That ain't gonna happen. People say, I'm not against refugees, but I want them to follow the rules. My parents didn't follow the rules. They left in the middle of the goddamn night because they thought they were gonna get killed. You think I'm not going to try to go over the border and risk my life? So rules, schmules. You're going to do what you need to do. The rules are broken.

While those in Toronto did not evoke a history of the city as a place of resistance, emphasis was often placed on individual migration histories and an idea that the people within the city were representative of a norm of mobility that was not reflected in federal and provincial policies. Again, this reflects the recurring description of the sanctuary city in Toronto that was based on recent histories of migration and the centrality of migration for the future wealth of the city.

In San Francisco, finding justice in broken rules was expressed through abolitionism. Maria, a social worker for the San Francisco School District, explained how her understanding of sanctuary was entwined with understanding white supremacy and working towards racial equity,

> Sanctuary is an opportunity to remind staff of why we centre racial equity because if we don't get through that, none of this other stuff is going to be resolved.

All systems of detention and deportation are founded on anti-blackness. All of our law enforcement prison industrial complex all of those were born out of slavery and Jim Crow. So I try to bring it into this work to try to bring it into our relationships with our students, the community, government and law enforcement.

Ah-Lam, an undocumented sanctuary actor in San Francisco similarly based her narrative for working on sanctuary within abolitionist aims,

Sanctuary is about changing the system to create protection for the community. As a directly affected person, I may not have the paperwork but I am engaged in social citizenship and political citizenship. I am part of this community whether or not I have legal status. Sanctuary is about protecting *that* community. And for that you have to change the system. The vision around sanctuary is incomplete because the police and Board of Supervisors are coming at it from a different angle and that angle is primarily based on upholding a system that is based on white supremacy.

In Toronto, abolitionism was evident in some discussions between activists but was also linked to calls for indigenous sovereignty. Sanctuary was not an answer to this much broader reality even though activists were aware of its potential for reframing debates. As Swati, a human rights lawyer in Toronto, stated, 'the idea that we're Canadians, right, more than somebody else is, is a bit of a fallacy to me—talk to indigenous people'. While the notion of indigenous sovereignty might hold the most fundamental challenge and potential to think differently about precaritised residents, it did not build popular consensus even within those who organised for the sanctuary city and therefore could not be mobilised effectively.

In Sheffield, while there were those who were working on the boundaries of the rules to provide support to rejected asylum seekers, these activities were not underpinned with an abolitionist framework. Rather, the sphere of organising outside notions of humanitarianism were based on previous trade union activity and workers' rights, as Peter explained,

We build on our links with the Sheffield Trades Council. Saying to them that when people can't work they work illegally and they don't have unions, no health and safety, and drive down wages. So it's trying to build coalitions on the basis of solidarity and mutual interests.

In Sheffield these sanctuary actors were committed to anti-racist work; however, their basis for building solidarities was not through organising within this an abolitionist tradition and they did not mobilise narratives of white supremacy or invoke historical inequities to build common ground unlike in anti-racist organisations in Toronto and San Francisco.

Summing Up the 'Just City'

Narratives that invoked values of justice, equality, and fairness when mobilising the notion of the sanctuary city were more diverse and wider ranging than those that made up efficient or healthy city moral values. The notions of justice that built consensus for sanctuary reinforced contingent belonging through continuous probationary citizenship or humanitarian exception. However, sanctuary actors who mobilised these arguments were often reflective about their positions and the limitations posed by leveraging these values in practice. They were also keenly aware of the unsettling questions and dilemmas that emerged. Crucially, these unsettling questions were most clearly revealed through the practice of living daily life alongside those without secure legal status.

Some sanctuary actors came to an understanding that sanctuary could not be achieved without breaking rules. Here, city-level identity became salient as activists sought a 'barometer' for their actions, not within current legal frameworks but in the city's reimagined past. These memories of resistance were invoked in San Francisco and Sheffield. In Toronto, rather than conjuring memories of a resisting city, sanctuary actors drew on personal life histories of migration to understand their own position in relation to precaritised residents.

Final Remarks

There is remarkable diversity in the narratives mobilised by sanctuary actors. These differ not only across cities, institutions, and sanctuary actors but also across time, as previous histories and memories of sanctuary shift and are remembered anew. This chapter shows that there can be no overriding definition of a sanctuary city but rather emergent moral values of the sanctuary city whose different meanings are mobilised in different contexts to suit different ends. Moreover, as Muehlebach renders in fine-grained ethnographic detail and is mirrored here, 'progressive' moral orientations can end up supporting and sustaining systems of exploitation and inequality as much as challenging them (2012, 6–9).

These values come to form the common ground that sanctuary actors work within, and the potential directions that they envisage could broaden this common ground but are currently foreclosed. These include campaigns such as framing indigenous sovereignty alongside sanctuary or framing the neoliberalised city as an engine of inequality. These campaigns have not (yet) found the broad-based support needed on which to push effectively for precaritised residents' rights, perhaps because they signal a fundamental re-thinking of our notions of belonging which must also involve a reworking of the relationship between population, territory, and resources.

FIVE
Brokering Sanctuary
Practices of Knowledge and City Making

I think a groundswell is built up about what it's possible to say and what it's not possible to say. I think that moves the conversation in a committee meeting in a certain way. They're far less likely to say something in Sheffield that is directly going to harm people we're offering sanctuary to. And that would have a bite. They would have to really justify it. . . . On the other hand, it also stokes anti-migrant feeling. And then you get the reaction to the narrative such as why are you a City of Sanctuary? You are just encouraging all the anti-migrant stuff. It depends on how that balance can be negotiated.

Dave, Co-director of Sheffield migrant organisation

This chapter details the complex negotiations, renderings, and composing that take place in the making of the sanctuary city. It zooms in on one moment in each city when a new situation arose that threatened to fragment, in the words of Dave above, the 'balance' of the sanctuary city. Each of these moments emerged due to the shifting relationship between the city and the nation as the relationships between people, place, and resources were being reworked. The moments that I unfold in this chapter can be conceived as instances when deference to dominant or official narratives that work to reinstate policy ambitions and conceal divergent and contradictory logics are disrupted. In these instances we can learn about the 'black boxing' of governance and in the words of Eric Wolf (1999, 126), 'they provide unusual insight into the functions of a complex system through a study of its dysfunctions' (see also Latour (1999, 304) on technology work that is made invisible through its own success). We can find meaning in these moments of tension, when there is friction, where governing systems momentarily seize up and new practices emerge. In these moments we can trace how moral values produce effects and what those effects can come to mean. The strength of this approach is that it makes possible a deeper analysis of how actors operate to stabilise interpretations and produce policy 'success'. I call these 'acts of brokerage'. As Clarke and colleagues (2015, 32) detail,

> Brokers do a lot of work. The cultural work of imagination (the problematizing, appropriation or borrowing of other policy framings, discourses and themes) the political work of articulation—vocalising different perspectives, building alliances, and aligning interests and constituencies; the organisational work of coordination—crafting the discourses, techniques and technologies that try to ensure implementation compliance and commitment and the work of translating giving the policy life and meaning as it moves from context to context.

Those who undertake brokering acts have an in-depth knowledge of their embedded context and the room for manoeuvre within their city-level governing systems. They operate within networks of actors who hold different moral values about the sanctuary city. They work with the different meanings and potentials from moral values that are circulating in the institutional or organisational languages of different stakeholders and use them to create interest and make sanctuary real. It is through this complex and unending work that various actors make up the sanctuary city.[1]

This chapter elucidates how possibilities that hold radical potential become re-signified as local government amalgamates them into state machinery. In the face of these processes sanctuary advocates face difficult choices. They can work with these systems or outside them. Acts of brokerage emerge as crucial in translating between these registers. Sanctuary brokers worked with the promise of liberal citizenship; situating themselves as working towards a more equal society in practice that will deliver the vision of liberal democracy in law. They shaped radical politics into something that can be incorporated into local government that is feasible, palatable, and keeps all elements of the state machinery intact. The chapter explores one brokering moment in San Francisco, Sheffield, and Toronto before concluding with the insights that can be gained from asking questions across each of these cities and their embedded practices of the sanctuary city.

San Francisco: Defending Sanctuary Against 'Bogeymen'

The sanctuary moment that helps to elucidate how moral values produce effects in San Francisco emerged in January 2019. Key acts of brokerage were undertaken by Joanne, a human rights lawyer, alongside the larger network of sanctuary actors in San Francisco. The context for the case is as follows. 'Azaza', a Tunisian national, was accused of raping an unconscious, intoxicated woman he picked up while working as a taxi driver in San Francisco. A no-bail warrant for his arrest was issued in June 2018, and he fled to Canada, where he was arrested. To extradite him, the Department of Homeland Security (DHS) was required to grant temporary parole to enter the United States to stand trial. The issue arose because following the passing of SB54 (the 'California Sanctuary Act'), DHS included a new parole condition. This condition stated that whatever the verdict, the Sheriff's office would inform DHS if the defendant was released from custody. This contravened San Francisco's Sanctuary Ordinance, which stated that unless the defendant has a previous felony conviction and is charged with another felony they will not be reported to DHS. Azaza had no previous felony convictions and, therefore, if he were acquitted, under the Sanctuary Ordinance the Sheriff could not report him to DHS.

The case gained media attention when the issue moved from an internal District Attorney (DA) legal decision to a legislative issue for the Board of Supervisors. The DA's office wrote a piece of legislation that would allow them to contravene the Sanctuary Ordinance in this circumstance. They submitted this to the Clerk of the Board on 7 January 2019; it was assigned to the Rules Committee on 15 January and was passed as amended on 23 January.[2] It was then moved to the Board of Supervisors for a decision on 29 January 2019. Azaza was transferred on 27 January 2020. On 28 January DHS dropped the condition and so there was no need for the Board of Supervisors to decide. The amendment was tabled until further notice at the hearing on 29 January.

I became aware of the case in an interview with Joanne on 28 January. When I arrived at her plush legal offices in downtown San Francisco, she offered me tea and cookies and asked if I needed to use the bathroom, noting that she remembered how tiring she found her Master's fieldwork in the UK. The offices were decorated with posters from the civil and human rights campaigns that this legal organisation had supported. At this stage, Joanne did not know Azaza had already been transferred and DHS had dropped the condition. In my notes from that interview, I wrote Joanne was a 'real linchpin of the movement' because she presented herself as holding an encyclopaedic knowledge of the legal issues and sanctuary advocacy since 2008 and had long-standing relationships with activists, faith organisations, legislative aides, and elected officials both at municipal and state level (Humphris 2021). Joanne's moral values had shifted throughout this time,

> I have tried every incremental and transitional approach I can think of in the last 14 years and the system recreates itself. We have spent years training police not to be racist, but that does not stop officer involved shootings of people of color. That's a lesson learned. A lot of human rights advocates are grappling with decades of a transitional approach and how little it's gotten us.

She went on to describe how she uses abolitionism as her 'guiding light'. This purposiveness, even if it may not be achieved or provokes decisions that have unintended consequences, is a transformative power and potential of sanctuary cities. Joanne relied on a large network of sanctuary actors. The immigrants' rights community had spent the morning before our interview visiting Supervisors and making sure the issue did not become a technical detail but was politicised and linked to the federal government agenda. She explained,

> Today we were meeting with each Supervisor that we could get a meeting with and explaining the history of sanctuary and although extradition is a really unique situation the testing is really the same and the concerns about due process are still there. We pointed out to them that this is all concocted and manufactured. This is a reality that they just created 10 months ago. It didn't go through any legislative or public process so please let's not legislate based on that. Let's put on our thinking caps and be aware and not passively accept something from a bully but be creative and fight and resist and all this stuff that people give a lot of lip service to but let's actually do it and act on it and have guts.

She was also coordinating her work with other advocates. She continued, 'so when I was at City Hall today, I was talking about the legal technicalities of this ordinance and how that intersects with sanctuary. Separately the faith community were doing the same. I ran into them in the hallways, and they were talking to the Supervisors on the point of their values'. The coordinated response from lawyers and faith advocates both delineated the moral problem and provided creative legal solutions and political narratives in an interactive process with elected politicians.

Joanne argued DHS could not change their practice without some form of official oversight. As she described, 'It's merely a letter. It's not a warrant, a federal law, it's not a regulation, and it doesn't even appear to be a contract. It's a thing that is really about let's do each other favours'. She also argued the DA's office did not push back hard enough against this condition. She does not accept a notion of federal power as fixed and permanent but as fluctuating and contestable. She acts to personalise federal policies, placing them back within the play of local relations.

The alternative perspective was put forward by the DA's office. I interviewed Nicole, a DA official, in her office on 2 February; the meeting started late and was cut short by her assistant because Nicole had an urgent call. In the thirty minutes we shared, she clarified the conflict between federal and municipal government, 'DHS are totally entitled to do whatever they want. If you take the energy of sanctuary out of it from a purely governing functioning place there is logic to it. They are saying we are going to take the risk of bringing someone to this country who doesn't have a right to be in this country to face an accusation of a very serious crime. And if they get released out into the community we would like to know'. Nicole also explained that they had not taken the decision lightly and have explored other avenues, 'extradition is a lengthy process. There were months where at the staff level people were dealing with it before we were aware of a real collision of our values'. She continued, 'the number of things that complicated it and made it impossible to find other avenues was a little comical.[3] We talked to the US attorney's office we talked to DOJ [Department of Justice]. We exhausted everything'.

The sticking point for the DA was their mandated duty to bring someone to trial and to seek 'true justice and to support crime survivors'. As Nicole described, 'We tried not to do it [sign the letter] and they [DHS] said OK we will just not bring him. And then Canada said fine we'll send him back to Tunisia if you don't come and pick him up. Which means we then don't prosecute his sexual assault. Our whole role is to bring justice and so we were in a very challenging situation of these competing values. And so, the City Attorney said we need permission from the Board of Supervisors'. This explanation illustrates how criminality and the corresponding moralities attached were blurred with Azaza's migration status.

The issue was moved from a technocratic sphere into the political and public domain. Nicole believed it was the right decision because the DA didn't have the authority to break the Sanctuary Ordinance but equally, they would not be upholding their city-mandated role if they didn't pursue a trial. However, many Supervisors did not agree that the DA should have brought the contravention of the Sanctuary Ordinance to them.

Cyrus, a recently elected San Francisco Supervisor, believed it was not the Board's role to adjudicate on these cases. In an interview in his office in City Hall accompanied by his legislative aide who was also writing notes about our conversation he explained to me, 'I think I've been very vocal and very clear that you can never ever undermine sanctuary policy and shame on the federal government and shame on the DA's office for even making that an issue'. He uses conflicting moralities to account for himself in an interactive process in which he is trying to mobilise support for his key issue of civil rights. He continues, 'once you set a precedent for change then you open the floodgates. So who is to say that the DA wouldn't be asking us to do that in every case now that involved an undocumented immigrant. I always look at the example of Kamala Harris when she ran for DA and she ran on a platform that was heavily against the death penalty and as soon as she got elected a police officer was killed and everybody was very upset that she would not seek the death penalty. You can't stand for something and then when it gets hard go against that'.

Joanne explained to me that she had linked the sanctuary city to his ability to get re-elected and his political career. She described how he supported her interpretation from the outset because he clearly linked this issue to civil rights, which was the argument he used to get elected. She had solidified this link and provided Cyrus with further interpretations. In particular, he draws not on the history of sanctuary but on previous political figures (Kamala Harris) who had to stand by their election promises. Joanne explained to me that she often uses the future political ambitions of those in elected office as a mode to compose and give power to her interpretation of the contemporary moment and in doing so mobilises others in the pursuit of her understanding of sanctuary policy (while demobilising others such as the DA).

The agenda item came to the floor of the Board of Supervisors on 29 January[4] even though Azaza had already been transferred and DHS had dropped the condition. Three supervisors used this opportunity not only to reiterate their perspective and commitment to the sanctuary city but also as a platform to publicly perform San Francisco's moral ground.[5] Supervisor Ronan,[6] who represents the largely Latinx District 9, linked the 'games' that the DHS were playing with San Francisco with the 'games' the DHS under the instruction of the then President Donald Trump were playing with children on the US border with Mexico, in a highly emotive and impassioned speech.

Supervisor Fewer talked directly to the camera of this recorded public meeting. She tied her comments back to the role of San Francisco as a moral compass, not only for the USA, but also 'the world',

> In San Francisco we stand for something. In San Francisco people look to us. If we chip away at our sanctuary law, the rest of the United States looks at us too. We stand strong, so they can stand strong. We have a bigger responsibility than our jurisdiction in San Francisco. We have a responsibility to the rest of the United States and to the world.

After this speech several people in the gallery cheered and raised their hands in appreciation (including the minute taker). The chair of the Board of Supervisors added that he had 'slipped on the slope' and was glad that his colleagues 'picked me up'. As they spoke Joanne sat in the audience alongside other members of the wider sanctuary network including a legislative aide of one Supervisor and two long-standing members of advocacy group 'Free SF'. Three members of the faith-based organising network 'Faith in Action' were also in the audience. They had visited Supervisors the previous morning to persuade them not to vote for this amendment in accordance with their values. They had pushed Supervisors on the issue of separating families and the children being detained by the federal government on the US–Mexico border. At the end of the meeting, I talked to Joanne on the steps of the City Hall, and I asked whether she was satisfied with the speeches. She replied, 'everyone in San Francisco is going to say they're pro-immigrant but that doesn't dictate how they are going to land on something like extradition. And that really tests you and your values. That's when people fall apart. Even a politician that markets themselves as progressive in San Francisco can still say— this case is really bad. To me that speaks to the host-guest relation'. Joanne was clear that residence was still contingent and therefore the often-repeated claims that undocumented residents were legitimate and equal members of the city were not realised.

Sanctuary actors undertook many acts of brokerage to corral three supervisors to position themselves within their interpretation of the sanctuary city. They pushed different leverage points with each Supervisor, appealing to civil rights, religious convictions, and their political careers to de-mobilise the public safety narrative of the DA's office and their blurring of criminality with immigration. In different ways, sanctuary actors persuaded Supervisors that maintaining their interpretation of the sanctuary city was the 'right' and the 'good' thing to do. They were also persuaded that this decision would not have economic costs for the city because of a separate development that was happening in the Ninth Circuit Appeal Court located a short walk away from San Francisco's City Hall. On 25 January 2017 within five days of Donald Trump's inauguration as President, he issued 'Enhancing Public Safety in the Interior of the United States (EO 13768), which was swiftly followed by a DHS memorandum, 'Enforcement of the Immigration Laws to Serve the National Interest'. The Executive Order specifically targets 'sanctuary jurisdictions'. In Section 9, it states 'jurisdictions that wilfully refuse to comply with 8 U.S.C. 1373 [addressing information sharing regarding immigration and citizenship status between government agencies and the Immigration and Naturalization Service] are not eligible to receive Federal grants, except as deemed necessary for law enforcement purposes.' In response, on 31 January 2017, the City and County of San Francisco filed in the US District Court (Northern District of California), asking the court to declare Section 9(a) unconstitutional. Following almost two years of legal proceedings the Ninth Circuit ruled that the federal government could not withhold the grants and therefore the Supervisors were protected from any backlash about losing federal funds.

Crucially, in San Francisco (which was not evident in any other city), sanctuary actors were able to mobilise moral values maintaining their interpretations of sanctuary as the moral course of action through the risk to elected members that they might be on the wrong side of history when they make decisions about the sanctuary policy. This narrative gained currency when Gavin Newsom, former Mayor of San Francisco, apologised for his policy of deporting undocumented children when he became California Governor (A. Hart 2018). Many politicians in San Francisco aimed for (and have a history of) gaining office in higher levels of government. Sanctuary actors used notions of justice to broker with elected city officials aided by their aspirations for their political futures. Furthermore, the wider sanctuary city activist network was able to link the highly emotive subject of the treatment of children at the US–Mexico border, with the federal government's attack on sanctuary cities. Crucially, this reframed the question away from the extradition of a person accused of rape, to the separation of families. More radical claims that rested on principles of equality for all, were sidelined in favour of arguments about the deservingness of migrant families. This argument was more palatable to the municipal government. In San Francisco, networks of actors worked together and pushed elected officials with a united goal. These shared values were not evident in Sheffield and led to very different acts of brokerage.

Sheffield: Shifting 'Welcome' to 'Non-cooperation'?

In Sheffield, similarly to San Francisco, a moment of tension emerged that required acts of brokerage as the sanctuary city was being used to mobilise different understandings towards very different ends. The sanctuary moment was sparked when the migrant advocacy group, SYMAAG, uncovered a funding application from the municipal government to national government's 'Controlling Migration Fund' scheme. They mounted a case against the municipal government for applying for funding from the Home Office to resource new private housing officers who would report tenants to UK Border Force officers. The advocacy group argued that this contravened Sheffield's self-designation as a City of Sanctuary because they were cooperating with the national government's policy that would result in residents being detained and deported. The tension centred on the definition and meaning of City of Sanctuary in the UK's hostile environment. It is important to note that City of Sanctuary is not only municipal government's self-designation but also an organisation ('City of Sanctuary Sheffield' or CoSS) located in a building called 'The Sanctuary' (see Humphris 2020).

Acts of brokerage were crucial in translating between the advocacy group's radical challenge to the municipal government and the longer-standing practice and definition of the City of Sanctuary in Sheffield. The events unfolded as follows. On 8 August 2019 SYMAAG posted a blog entitled 'Sheffield: Hostile Environment or City of Sanctuary?' (SYMAAG 2019) and laid out a challenge to the local government. The blog was provoked by a report to the Director of Housing and Neighbourhoods Service regarding the approval of the grant application. The report dated 11 March 2019 included several sentences that SYMAAG interpreted as the municipal government colluding with Home

Office enforcement. Through this blog, SYMAAG redefined City of Sanctuary as non-cooperation, rather than, as was currently the case, defined as 'welcome'. They referred to other local governments (not necessarily cities of sanctuary) who passed resolutions of non-cooperation with central government's hostile environment policies.[7] This comparison sought to identify the ways that some local governments had already begun practices of non-cooperation, even though Sheffield's municipal government claimed that there was no room for manoeuvre to resist central government's legislative agenda.

SYMAAG presented their case to the Refugee and Migrant Forum in August 2019. They also held an open public planning meeting on Tuesday 17 September and held a demo on 19 September before making a petition to the Safer and Stronger Communities Scrutiny Committee. Dave was a member of this committee as the chair of an NGO called 'Cohesion Sheffield' (CS). He wrote a response paper to SYMAAG's petition. In this paper, which he shared with me for comment, Dave translated SYMAAG's concerns, taming the language and organising priorities, noting 'the petition raises important issues that need to be discussed, but CS advises we take a more nuanced and collaborative approach'. Dave curated SYMAAG's perspectives into policy actions that could be digested by the municipal government. The paper did not agree with SYMAAG's complaint about the Controlling Migration Fund, but they agreed that SYMAAG had 'surfaced several key issues'. Dave moved the issues raised away from political debate and focused on process and bureaucratic technicalities including the municipal government's need to define who their proposed partner agencies were and whether they ensured that appropriate support was put in place if 'vulnerable individuals' were identified. Dave used strategic language that moved away from the term 'illegal immigrants' and placed tenants without a migration status in frames of humanitarianism and vulnerability.

He also identified that an Equality Impact Assessment had not been conducted. The municipal government responded, referring to reports to the Director of Housing & Neighbourhoods (11 March and 8 August 2019) that both state, 'The Council is not required to consult on this proposal' and that an Equality Impact Assessment is not necessary because 'accepting the grant will not directly impact anyone or anything that supports the services that are accessed by our customers/tenants etc.'. Dave identified that the Council must extend their equality duty to all residents of Sheffield and not only council tenants and customers. Here, Dave embarks on a similar reworking and broadening of duties of the city that was undertaken in Toronto, not to citizens but to all residents, leveraging the notion of equality enshrined in liberal democratic citizenship. However, Dave did not have the legal backing of the City Solicitor and this interpretation did not hold. This is an important point because it indicates how embedded context shapes how moral values produce effects and what those effects can come to mean. It also reveals the importance of networks of actors working together to broker new meanings.

The CS report also requested further information about the possible collusion between South Yorkshire Police and the UK Border Force. They recommended a full policy review was conducted so all members of municipal government are clear on what was and what was not to be reported. Crucially, Dave identified CoSS should lead the review because 'otherwise others are defining what a City of Sanctuary is'.[8] Here, Dave reworked the priority of stakeholders, reshaped the problem and in doing so tamed the radical potential of SYMAAG by placing them outside the review. In this way, he formed a palatable solution for municipal government.

To diffuse the radical potential of SYMAAG's claims, the municipal government gave weak commitments that they would stop the reporting, but with no oversight or structural changes to the private housing department or the police. Moreover, the municipal government argued that different Sheffield organisations involved in supporting and campaigning for migrants' rights had different views about what 'City of Sanctuary' should mean, driving a wedge between CoSS and SYMAAG. They argued that they would only consider a change of meaning when civil society organisations were united in their approach. By making the issue bureaucratic and technical (an issue for the housing department's equality policy) and displacing the debate onto civil society, the municipal government successfully diffused the radical challenge to shift their definition of City of Sanctuary from a broad and vague commitment to 'welcome' to a more concrete policy of 'non-cooperation'.

This moment highlights several key issues shaping Sheffield's sanctuary city. The meaning of sanctuary had the potential to shift from 'welcoming' to 'non-cooperation', but sanctuary actors were not united in this meaning or the means through which to achieve it. We can identify clearly how different moral values came into conflict. CoSS believed in what has been called 'quiet politics' (Askins 2015; Sheringham and Taylor 2022) rather than SYMAAG's

racial justice aims, and the two groups saw these positions as mutually exclusive. Dave acted to mobilise CoSS, highlighting aspects relating to the
'efficient city' moral value while demobilising SYMAAG's notions of radical
justice. While Dave's intention was to encourage the migrant and asylum
seeker sector to come to a unified standpoint, the lack of leadership from CoSS
and the already fragmented and negative associations with the notion of sanctuary from other organisations in the sector (including SYMAAG) meant that
he brokered to open a space that was unable to be filled.

The case also reveals the fragile moral values of Sheffield's sanctuary city.
I quoted Dave at the beginning of this chapter and his description of how the
sanctuary city designation has the potential to mobilise both pro-migrant
and anti-migrant sentiment. He described himself as the 'conscience of the
council' to help elected members navigate these complexities. His description
of trying to 'balance' these conflicting moral values reveals the opportunities
and challenges of the sanctuary city. In contrast to San Francisco where the
sanctuary city could be used by elected officials to gain political currency,
the opposite was true in Sheffield due to the growing far-right presence. Dave
therefore sought to make this issue technocratic and not open to public debate
where elected members would have to openly state they were supporting residents without a full legal migration status. Moreover, Dave's picking up of the
distinction between residents and tenants indicates one of the ways in which
citizenship is diminished and incorporated at a municipal level. Finally, compared to San Francisco, Sheffield was exposed in a relationship with a strong
central (and centralising) national government without the cover of intermediary institutions in a federal governing system. It was more difficult in a unitary governing system to separate a municipal duty of care from the national
duty of care, decreasing their room for manoeuvre.

Toronto's Shelter 'Crisis': Firewalls 'On the Fly'

In Toronto, similarly to San Francisco and Sheffield, we see a moment of tension brokered to shape the meaning and practice of the sanctuary city. The
key events in this sanctuary moment are as follows. In 2017, after the Trump
administration announced plans to withdraw temporary protected status for
individuals living in the US, Canada saw a large increase in people crossing
the southern border to claim asylum. Numbers rose from 433 between February and March 2017 to a peak of 8,559 between July and September 2017.

Numbers continued to be in the thousands rather than hundreds until the global Covid-19 pandemic when there was a sharp drop below 200.[9] Toronto began seeing an increase of arrivals into their shelter system in the summer of 2018. The cost of shelters for new arrivals was not covered by federal or provincial legislation and therefore had to be paid by municipal funds.[10]

The liberal federal government was supportive of new arrivals. Considering federal elections in October 2019, Prime Minister Trudeau publicly distinguished Canada from the Trump administration.[11] In contrast, the conservative Premier of Ontario, Doug Ford, was publicly anti-immigrant and had begun to dismantle and defund support for new arrivals, such as severely cutting legal aid for asylum claims. In addition, the Mayor of Toronto, John Tory, had long-standing animosity with Ford, coming to a head in 2018 when the provincial government unilaterally decided to slash the size of Toronto council from 47 to 25 councillors and announced swathing funding cuts to the City's budget. In this context, in October 2019, the municipal government was negotiating to sign a new Memorandum of Understanding (MoU) with the federal government (Immigration, Refugees and Citizenship Canada, IRCC). This represented a new policy instrument as the IRCC had not previously directly funded a municipality, effectively leap-frogging the anti-immigrant provincial government. Issues arose because IRCC required demographic data of those receiving funds. This contravened Toronto's Sanctuary Ordinance not to collect or share migration status information. The city government faced a tension between a crippling budget deficit and adherence to the Sanctuary Ordinance.

On 20 September 2019, I arranged an interview with Duncan, the director of the shelter system in Toronto. He greeted me warmly and with an infectious energy as he led me from the waiting area of the large bureaucratic building through open plan offices. As we entered his office and he took his place behind a large desk piled with papers, I noticed a large white board with Toronto in the centre and many other towns and organisations circling around it. During the interview Duncan referred to this white board. It depicted the plan to move people out of the shelter system in Toronto to the surrounding towns because of the lack of 'appropriate' accommodation in the city. He explained how the shelter crisis unfolded,

> We have a lot of irregular migration happening over the border. I'd say about 70% of the folks I'm serving on a nightly basis, are irregular crossers. Twenty

families a day are arriving in Toronto looking for the service. We've served 13,000 unique individuals since the beginning of 2018.

The boundaries around what is considered legitimate treatment of these new arrivals to the city is intrinsically entwined with funding and, crucially, the multi-level governance of the city and funding sources. The MoU with the federal government would provide additional resources to fund the shelter system.

This MoU was the subject of my interview with Andrew, a well-known, retired, high-ranking, non-elected municipal officer. After his retirement the previous year he had begun to work for a large social justice think tank in Toronto. I met him at this organisation on 29 October in a glass-walled meeting room where we spent five minutes talking about Michael Ondaatje's book *In the Skin of a Lion* before moving to the sanctuary city policy. I asked him about his understanding of what had become known as the 'shelter crisis',

Usually about 10% of the population at any given time are refugees in Toronto. That went up to 25%. Massive costs for the city, closer to $100 million annual coming from the property tax base. Then the Conservative government got elected in Ontario and wanted to go to war, and looked for any good reason to go to war with the liberal government in Ottawa, and immigration, particularly irregular migrants, became the perfect flashpoint.

Andrew described the political tensions for Toronto which were also entwined with notions regarding what were legitimate practices in treating these new arrivals. He explained,

Toronto was in a tough spot because we have no problem with irregular migrants arriving in the city. It's not our business, whether they are irregular or convention refugees or permanent residents. These are people arriving to make Toronto their home. And we have to respond.

It is here that Andrew's previous understanding and definition of sanctuary emerged (see Humphris 2020). In 2007, Andrew had reimagined the definition of the city to mean its residents rather than formal citizens. Andrew's framing of the city and its responsibilities was reinvoked here, highlighting the importance of long-standing relations and institutional knowledge that shaped brokering opportunities about these arrivals from the outset. Andrew continued,

> It was a challenging play. Because we didn't want to take sides. We wanted the Feds to cough up. But we didn't want to align with the Province. That really put the Feds in a difficult spot because they basically had never funded irregular migrants. It was extremely complicated . . . you've got this kind of role realignment happening on the fly.

Similarly to the other two cities, this destabilising of the sanctuary city occurred ad hoc as the relationship between different levels of government was being tested and renegotiated. The city was faced with a large budget deficit but a sanctuary ordinance that would not allow the acceptance of federal government resources because of their data-sharing conditions. Sanctuary brokers mobilised previous relationships fostered with the IRCC which was in debt to Toronto for resettling most Syrian refugees. Andrew explained,

> I was the bureaucratic lead on the Syrian issue, and it certainly built good relationships, both the bureaucratic and the political level, between Toronto and Canada. We made Canada look very good. Toronto very much saved the federal government's butt.

Personal relations gave Andrew room for manoeuvre to rework the sanctuary ordinance while also ameliorating the City's budget deficit through a firewall policy. In a similar way to Joanne, Andrew used his long-standing connections to personalise the issue and to reframe it as a negotiation between equals working with sets of regulations rather than seeing power as emanating from the federal government in a hierarchy. He described how he leveraged the Access T.O. Ordinance within these conversations,

> In that initial discussion with IRCC about data, I said, guys, here's the Access T.O. policy. Whatever we do, you must, in blood, tell me there's a firewall between you and CBSA. If you can't give us that, we have no conversation.

They agreed to the firewall because, as Andrew describes, 'they didn't have a choice'. He continued,

> They had a new Premier who wanted to go to war with them from the largest, most powerful province in the country. They're trying to manage that. And they were heading to an October 2019 federal election. They would have lost in the

court of public opinion if they had tried to force us, and they couldn't have survived that. And it would have given another plank to the Province to beat them over the head with. So they agreed. A lot of the IRCC bureaucrats were thrilled that Toronto was saying you have to agree there is no cooperation with CBSA.

As well as reading interests and composing a balance in line with the municipal sanctuary ordinance, sanctuary brokers gave the IRCC a justification based on the city's moral values for the department not to cooperate with CBSA. The outcome of these acts of brokerage was a reconfigured relationship between the municipality and the federal government. While there were federally funded programmes, the primary funding relationship for the municipality was with the province. This MoU represented a new policy precedent where the municipality could be directly funded from the federal government.

Access T.O. was leveraged in several ways. First, it stipulated the municipality was not concerned with the legal status of those who arrive in Toronto. The municipality also upheld the value of free movement within Canada (so people could freely arrive). Therefore, those arriving in Toronto were treated as any other resident of the city and provided with shelter. Second, the Access T.O. Ordinance was leveraged across different levels of government. A wider network of actors from the municipal government (Social Development, Finance & Administration Division, SDFA) and the federal government (IRCC) had built relations of trust and shared values of justice for new arrivals that were not held in other federal government departments (CBSA) or by the provincial government of that time. Sanctuary brokers drew on these good relationships, taking advantage of the context of the federal election in October 2019.

Third, Toronto was framed as 'stepping up' both in the Syrian Crisis and in the response to new arrivals from the USA. Access T.O. was invoked to 'tame' the conservative members of Council in a similar way to the role played by the City of Sanctuary designation in Sheffield described by Dave. As Duncan explains,

> Our new provincial government started saying these are illegal people. Having a policy like Access T.O. in place, as a foundation to our view of this issue, tames down our City Council and individual politicians' ability to use that same language. This is a huge budget pressure on the city. It could quite easily become

a public political conversation at Council. And it really doesn't. If it did, you've got another Counsellor saying, wait a minute, our position is this. It really shuts down the conversation.

While Andrew brokered a deal that solved the City's budget deficit, it did so by not treating all urban residents equally. Irregular border crossers were evicted from Toronto shelters and forcibly moved out of Toronto to become the responsibility of those other jurisdictions (none of which had similar legislation to Access T.O.). This case demonstrates how the promise of equality that is held within the idea of the sanctuary city, was used to deepen inequalities, as municipal governments used it as a tool to move irregular borders crossers out of the city. The radical potential was thus extinguished, and nothing changed in the way the municipality worked.

Final Remarks

In the three moments described above, sanctuary actors exhibit a broad range of knowledge and skills including an in-depth understanding of political and moral economies within their cities and beyond. They have extensive knowledge of these systems, interpret symbols and meanings from one frame of reference to another, mediate across incompatibilities, and endeavour to build bridges or establish linkages across different viewpoints. They also are deeply invested in trying to solve, in the words of Andrew, 'a complex play', where delicate work is needed to create and balance interests to make sanctuary real.

One way to make sense of these different actions and their effects is through moral values. By tracing different moral values, how they produce effects and what those effects come to mean, we can understand why different sanctuary actors make different strategic decisions and the effects of those decisions in practice. For example, in San Francisco, linking the extradition of an alleged sex offender to the injustice of putting children in cages at the US–Mexico border allowed sanctuary actors to provide Supervisors with a justification for sanctuary that resonated with the City's history of social justice campaigns, rather than public safety. In Toronto, Andrew maintained the city government's position that they have a duty of care for all municipal residents and not only national citizens, relying on Toronto's record of being an efficient and capable city to manage new arrivals. Sanctuary actors specifically kept the issue within the technocratic sphere as a key point of leverage was to ensure that the province did not use the budget deficit in Toronto to stoke anti-migrant fears in the run up to the federal elections. In Sheffield, the lack of a united vision between conflicting moral values enabled the municipality to diffuse the challenge to their sanctuary city status. The sanctuary moment in Sheffield also foregrounds the difference between a federal and unitary government where cities' room for manoeuvre is curtailed due to the lack of intermediary institutions. It also highlights the importance of a united sanctuary city movement that rests on intersectional solidarity.

In addition, by focusing on how different moral values play out we can foreground the ever-changing nature of the sanctuary city, perceive sanctuary actors as contextually situated, and understand how sanctuary policy acts on and through these different actors. In each of these sanctuary moments the messiness of policy was revealed. Sanctuary policy was often made up without planning, preparation, or forethought. In these sanctuary moments there was a need to hastily solve a complex problem and creatively construct a solution that was improvised while also continuing the process of governing with all state machinery intact.

Moreover, a crucial similarity in these moments is the relation between the municipality and the federal government which was tied together with budgetary considerations. In San Francisco, federal government threatened to 'defund' cities who did not comply with ICE. In Sheffield, a condition of national government Home Office funding was for city-level housing officers to report those without legal migration status. In Toronto, federal government required the data of those receiving federal funds for accommodation, contravening Access T.O. This chapter has described the different strategies used by sanctuary actors in these moments to redefine what the sanctuary city means. In addition, through their practices they are also reshaping the relation between the city and the nation-state. Through this perspective the moral values of sanctuary cities can be conceived as struggles over sovereignty.

As this chapter demonstrates, sanctuary is not a status that can be achieved but is in a constant state of becoming. As Joanne explained, 'You're never going to be done. You never "win" sanctuary'. The stakes of the sanctuary city are most clearly revealed in times of perceived 'crisis' such as high-profile raids, a global pandemic, or when the national government acts outside prevailing moral values (e.g. Sensenbrenner Bill or threats of mass deportations). However, these actions do not always result in a reinvigoration of the sanctuary city. Sanctuary actors work hard to achieve their version of sanctuary cities. The sanctuary city is given meaning in these moments when it is linked to a broader threat or wider campaign. The sanctuary city therefore cannot be seen within a linear development or 'progress' because sanctuary actors respond to specific contexts.

The strength of this perspective lies in its capacity to highlight the ambiguous logics and values that guide and sustain the sanctuary city, by looking at the dynamic fields of struggle around the boundaries of what is good and acceptable, their power hierarchies, and the political projects they might inform. The book has interrogated the manifold interactions between national identity politics and liberal democratic notions of welcome, hospitality, and compassion; the (re)emergence of the sovereignty of cities and increasing inland border enforcement; widening inequalities and inability of the post-welfare neoliberal state to redistribute resources in late capitalism; as well as structures of racialisation and white supremacy. The point, then, is not to establish a neat 'fit' or fixed conceptualisation of the interaction between these elements, but rather to reveal the tensions and contradictions that exist between different logics and processes. In this way we can tease out the potential of the sanctuary city for providing political contestation and alternative forms of solidarity while also tracing how those potentials may be extinguished as they are made palatable for city-level government. The book has described the emerging moral values of sanctuary practices that shift according to these tensions, including how 'progressive' policies are justified as a technology to maintain urban order and claim city sovereignty and how sanctuary actors contest the treatment of precaritised residents through moral claims.

CONCLUSION
A Moral for Urban Governance?

> Sanctuary status makes a huge difference to what I do because it is not just you fighting. You have the moral backing of the community. The moral support.
>
> Marco, San Francisco Public Defender

> Sanctuary is really easy. Everybody can posture for it. It imposes very few burdens on the people who run the show.
>
> Pat, Retired Civil Rights Activist, San Francisco

Which perspective on the sanctuary city is true? As this book has shown, it is both. This book has asked *why* the sanctuary city comes to be practised in one way or another and explored *how* this plays out on the ground. These questions allow the differences and tensions among and between sanctuary cities to be viewed not as a problem to be solved, but a source of meaning to be elaborated.[1] Only then can we come to greater understanding of what 'work' the sanctuary city is being used to do in a particular context. This approach challenges the notion that sanctuary cities are inherently antagonistic to national policies towards migration, settlement, and citizenship.[2] However, it does not write-off sanctuary cities as political branding or misplaced charity. As has been eloquently argued by previous scholars, sanctuary city policies operate within a contested political field that has just as much potential to reproduce entrenched hierarchies as challenge them (Darling 2010; Mancina 2018; Roy 2019). This book builds on this literature to provide the first comparative ethnographically informed reading of sanctuary cities that teases out the potential of sanctuary cities but also the complex processes through which governing systems extinguish practices animated by radical potential.

Sanctuary cities are given significance at a particular moment to address irreconcilable tensions in urban governance. These tensions can be traced back to the inception of cities as subsumed under nation-states. These tensions are exacerbated by the political complexities of governing a globalised city with limited sovereignty alongside economic growth imperatives and demand for low-wage labour; and increasing securitisation of migration alongside commitments to liberal citizenship rights and entitlements. One way to make sense of these tensions is through exploring moral values. By tracing different moral values, how they produce effects and what those effects come to mean we can understand why sanctuary actors make different strategic decisions and the effects of those decisions in practice. Brokering practices in moments where the sanctuary city was challenged hold the key to understanding the stakes of the sanctuary city, including its complex, contingent, and sometimes contradictory struggles. These moments also hold insights into liberal democratic citizenship, which holds emancipatory potential, but in practice can further institute inequalities. This analysis reveals how liberal citizenship is undermined by the very thing that makes it worth investing in—the promise of equality.

The Shape of Sanctuary Cities in San Francisco, Sheffield, and Toronto

This book has been dedicated to exploring the widely varying trajectories, aims, targets, significance, and resources across pioneering sanctuary cities in Canada, UK, and USA. The differences between the cities can be explained through several factors. First, the legal constitution and position of cities within the national governing framework fundamentally shapes sanctuary cities. The governing framework affects cities' ability to raise funds. San Francisco had the most latitude to raise funds, while Toronto and Sheffield had extremely limited mechanisms. In addition, San Francisco and Toronto, as cities in federalised nation-states, disavowed responsibilities that federal government endeavoured to bestow on the municipal government. They declared they had municipal duties to all urban residents rather than only to national citizens, broadening their room for manoeuvre. Crucially, when given the opportunity, SCC chose not to widen their duty of care from 'citizens' to 'residents' due to the unitary governing system, limiting the scope of the sanctuary city and the arguments that could be made to expand legitimate practices towards precaritised residents. This move, particularly in San Francisco, became politically and morally very powerful. In addition, residency goes beyond citizenship in important and distinctive ways, not least in restoring the urban as a site of affiliation and identification, against the nation.

Second, linked to the legal constitution of cities and flows of funding, is the importance of welfare state context. In San Francisco, the city extends rights and services into the gaps created by the complexity of the federal system. For example, Abigail, the Director of Social Security Programmes in San Francisco, described how gaps in federal resources provided an opening for the city, stating, 'adult services and elder care are typically not federally funded so we have more room here'. Similarly in Toronto, federalism allowed more room for manoeuvre by leaving gaps between federal, provincial or local reporting such as the opportunity for strategic framing (for instance 'medically uninsured', which included all newcomers to Ontario). In Sheffield, the unitary governing system and centralised service delivery constrained sanctuary cities' influence. Moreover, in the UK's hostile environment sanctuary cities can exacerbate restrictive national policies by monitoring and providing surveillance on precaritised residents.

The shape of the welfare state in each country also had effects for the efficacy of data-sharing mechanisms between federal and local government. For example, in Sheffield, due to the centralised publicly funded and publicly delivered healthcare system, the MoU between NHS Digital and the Home Office had immediate nationwide effects. Whereas in Toronto and San Francisco, the federal government had to make separate agreements across different states and provinces making data-sharing policies more difficult to roll out comprehensively. Furthermore, in the United States, Immigration and Customs Enforcement (ICE) makes separate 'Memoranda of Agreement' (known as 287g agreements) with state and local law enforcement agencies to delegate immigration enforcement authority to officers within the local agency, creating a patchwork of enforcement regimes across the country.[3] These agreements must be renewed providing an opening for advocacy and renewed scrutiny. These processes did not exist in the unitary and centralised UK Government context.

Third, the role of networks between government levels was also crucial to the shape of the sanctuary city. For example, many of those I interviewed in Toronto were previous members of the executive board for the Canadian Council for Refugees. This gave them access to high-ranking officials such as the national director of the Canadian Border Services Agency (CBSA). The

Canada-Ontario Immigration Agreement (COIA) as described in Chapter 3, also forged links between municipal and federal government. These connections became crucial to the sanctuary city, as municipal sanctuary actors could halt immigration raids or broker the establishment of firewalls. In San Francisco, many of those who held high office in the municipality moved up to the state or federal government. Relationships forged at the city level were leveraged at the state level to provide further legislative and ideological support to the sanctuary city. For example, a San Francisco coalition against Secure Communities relied on links with the San Franciscan-born Attorney General of California, Jerry Brown, leading to the Truth Act[4] and the Trust Act.[5] The previous Mayor of San Francisco, Gavin Newsom, became Governor of California and openly spoke out against Donald Trump's immigration policies. He apologised for his own policy of deporting undocumented youth in 2008 bolstering San Francisco's challenge to Trump's threat to sanctuary cities (Hart 2018). In contrast, Sheffield's sanctuary actors lacked these networks and when they did exist, they decreased Sheffield's room for manoeuvre. For example, David Blunkett, a Sheffield Member of Parliament, was also the British Home Secretary between 2001 and 2004. This relationship made it less likely that Sheffield would diverge from national government migration policy, rather Sheffield became the testing ground for national policies such as the Gateway Protection Programme.[6]

Fourth, how NGOs were funded made a difference. For example, in San Francisco private philanthropy (linked to a progressive political environment and rapidly growing economic context) meant that many human rights organisations that were fighting for migrants' rights were well funded and resourced. The municipal government had also made funds available to specifically protect precaritised residents in the city in the wake of the election of Donald Trump (Humphris 2021). In contrast, migrants' rights organisations in Toronto were fighting for increasingly limited funds as the provincial government cut budgets particularly legal aid. In response, a shadow network of support for precaritised residents was evident in Toronto. Some organisations' management allowed support workers to take on responsibilities for precaritised residents even though they could not be accounted for in their provincial or federal funded projects. In Sheffield, migrants' rights organisations fought over an extremely small amount of funding often relying on volunteers and fundraising efforts, creating competition and straining solidarity.

Fifth, a key difference emerged between the kinds of organisations and people supporting precarious status residents in each city and the histories of organising in each city. In San Francisco, and to a lesser extent Toronto, NGOs supporting undocumented residents were broader community or neighbour-hood-based organisations and not solely migrants' rights organisations. Many organisations were neighbourhood community centres serving all residents in the area. In San Francisco, many of those working in these organisations were not only born in the city, but in the neighbourhood where they worked (some now commuting for three hours because they could not afford to live in the city). Their primary motivation for their work were the residents in the area, and the sanctuary city had become one way they described parts of their work. These actors did not approach the notion of the sanctuary city as a par-ticular cause or interest, but as an integral part of their everyday lives along-side other community concerns, such as housing and eviction, food security or decent work. In contrast, some organisations in Toronto and all the organi-sations in Sheffield involved in the sanctuary city were solely migrant organ-isations. They included volunteers who wanted to support precarious status migrants as a form of charity or 'helping'. In Sheffield, those who worked in both a migrant-serving organisation and what they described as their own community organisation kept these two areas of work separate. These differ-ent positionings were crucial to how the sanctuary city policy acted on and through the subjectivity of different actors.

The relationship between 'sanctuary' and 'the political' differed hugely across the three cities indicating the importance of the relationship between demographics, histories of migration and settlement, and the political envi-ronment of the nation, region, and city. In San Francisco, those at the fore-front of sanctuary organising had taken on an understanding of politics that was close to the ideas of Black Feminist Thought (Hill Collins, 2010). While everyone I interviewed in San Francisco identified as supporting the Dem-ocratic Party, the sanctuary city was not always framed as a commitment to 'left-wing' politics but rather as a personal political commitment to commu-nity. Patricia Hill Collins argues the idea of 'community' has powerful polit-ical potential within the emotional sphere wherein people assert identities and foster collective action on issues of shared concern (Hill Collins 2010, 12). Laura, the migrant activist who I quoted at the beginning of this book, ex-plained that, for her, the sanctuary city was about 'protecting our community' and asking, 'who do we love?' Sanctuary actors often described the sanctuary city as part of being aware of their own positionalities, their roles, and the power they could leverage to further wider aims. As described by Maria in Chapter 4, 'sanctuary is part of a broader commitment to taking a personal inventory of positionalities around power and privilege and how that can be used to support precarious status residents'. Similarly, Lucy, director of social service programmes at a San Francisco community organisation, stated, 'I am a Black woman. I am aware of what I do with my power in this space. How I move that power in spaces and use it to interrupt systems is part of my understanding of sanctuary'. One effect of people connecting personally with these struggles was to organise in 'joint agency' (Kurnik and Razsa 2020) with precarious residents. This term has been used to describe the conjuncture of mobility struggles and local struggles, experiences, and traditions. 'Joint agency' stands in contrast to a 'need to help' (Malkki 2015).

In contrast, in Sheffield, CoSS employees and volunteers described their sanctuary work as 'non-political' or 'politically neutral'. This framing of neutrality dovetailed with the organisation's humanitarian ethos. However, this non-political stance caused tension between CoSS and other migrant organisations as reviewed in Chapter 5. The tension was not only because other organisations framed themselves as explicitly about 'left-wing politics' but also because of a perceived paternalistic culture of welcome that primarily framed precaritised residents as vulnerable. The sanctuary city was seen as something that people volunteered to do because they felt it was 'right', driven by a need to 'do something' in the face of national government hostility towards migrants. While this commitment was sometimes linked to wider community concerns and acknowledgement of positionalities and privileges, it did not change the underlying moral values that drove their actions.

In Toronto, those working under the notion of the sanctuary city during my fieldwork were primarily concerned with the technocratic aspects of the Access T.O. policy and implementation gaps. The sanctuary city's meaning had shifted from No One Is Illegal campaigns to the practical problems of implementing the Access T.O. policy at the frontline of service provision. There had been attempts to link the sanctuary city with the political economy of the city through the campaign 'The City is a Sweatshop'; however, campaigners lacked broad-based support and the campaign dwindled. As I was concluding my fieldwork in 2019, two grassroots organisations called 'Sanctuary Suppers' and S4 (The Sanctuary Students Solidarity Support Collective) had emerged that linked sanctuary to an ethics of care, notions of 'community building', and working in 'joint agency' that were reminiscent of sanctuary actors in San Francisco, but these organisations were nascent and under-resourced. These different understandings of politics shaped sanctuary city practices and how the sanctuary city could be brokered to (re)produce meanings. However, despite these wide-ranging differences, the sanctuary city 'succeeded' in becoming a mobilising metaphor in each country. What might the ubiquity of the sanctuary city across such different contexts indicate?

Why Sanctuary Cities Now?

Sanctuary cities may have become ubiquitous because organising has become more transnational. Policy geographers have argued for a notion of policy translation and mutation that includes movement across jurisdictions focusing on the actors' uneven power in policy networks (Peck 2011). Inspired by this literature I was attentive to where policy mutated across jurisdictions. For example, No One Is Illegal Toronto used San Francisco's municipal ID policy to campaign for a similar scheme in Toronto. Policy movement and translation also occurred between City of Sanctuary in the UK and an organisation called Welcoming America, which had a presence in San Francisco through the Chinatown YMCA. This helped me to understand a key difference between the UK and USA. In the UK, the sanctuary city concerns newly arrived asylum seekers whereas, in the USA, sanctuary cities include longer-standing residents who have been living in the city for generations.

Comparative policy ethnography also opened analysis to provide a further indication of why the sanctuary city has gained such a resonance in the contemporary moment and helps to explain why the sanctuary city became salient across different jurisdictions. All three national governments have adopted increasingly restrictive migration policies. It is ever-more complicated and expensive to gain and maintain a secure legal status and pass it on to children. Increasing numbers of people are becoming 'deportable' and status checks have become commonplace in everyday life. Inland border enforcement creates tensions for municipal government's institutional legitimacy because it is the lowest level of government and closest to urban residents. As residents with different migration statuses live together, have families, and entwine their everyday lives, the barriers between 'us' and 'them' break down and the assumed logic of differential treatment based on migration status loses its potency. In these instances, faith in governing institutions, which treated people differently based on migration status, was destabilised. For example, as Hannah described in Chapter 4, two young people whose lives had been extremely similar, were convicted of smoking marijuana. One received a warning, and the other was deported. Hannah described how the child who received a warning, and his classmates, began to question authority and the institutional legitimacy of governing institutions. She also described how she found it difficult as a parent to justify these decisions to her own children. In response, she shifted her moral values from incrementalism to abolitionism.

Inland border enforcement has unsettled the fragile balance that had been in place, which had allowed cities to manage, to some extent, their own legitimacy of governing. Focusing on these intractable dilemmas for urban policy makers and placing them within the longer history of the struggle for sovereignty between city and nation, reveals the stakes involved in the sanctuary city and the common challenge to all three cities. This longer history also helps to explain why the workings of the sanctuary city invokes such powerful moral tensions.

A further aspect of the sanctuary city that explains its contemporary significance is its role as a foil for tackling more radical claims based on racial justice or indigenous sovereignty. Activists were aware of the inability of the framework of the sanctuary city to bridge these issues, which also had an effect of undermining solidarity. For example, as Kelsey, a housing worker in San Francisco, stated, 'Black folks don't have the power base. No one talks about what our country is built on—Native Americans and Black folks. Sanctuary allows people to sideline other issues like structural racism'.

Lucy, the manager of social services in a Tenderloin community organisation in San Francisco, also raised the issue of animosity between communities because of local politicians' willingness to address sanctuary concerns but not broader structural issues that affect racialised low-income residents. She explains,

> When the Mayor takes a very strong stance on sanctuary—it felt like why wouldn't he take such a strong stance on gentrification and the displacement of African Americans in our community? It creates tension about who are we valuing, who gets the jobs, who gets access? There is a lot of tension between African Americans and Latinos.

Sanctuary actors were trying to bridge communities through common interests (such as eviction) but it did not gain momentum in municipal government and has not been included in municipal sanctuary city policies.

In Toronto, No One Is Illegal tried to expand the vision of what a sanctuary city could mean, particularly in relation to indigenous justice. As Nazir explained,

> We came up with the idea that there should be freedom to move, return and stay. And we explain it as a contradiction and a tension. How can you have freedom to stay between indigenous people and migrants? How can you have freedom to return in places that are now colonized?

While there was some support through the campaign group, No One Is Illegal on Stolen Lands, this was peripheral to the sanctuary city campaign and did not gain widespread support. Discussions about racial justice and indigenous sovereignty were not palatable for the municipal government and did not form the 'common ground' through which the sanctuary city could be brokered. Sanctuary cities allowed municipal governments to proclaim support for social justice without fundamentally transforming how government worked or the political or moral economies that sustained it.

Final Remarks

Sanctuary cities have been heralded as a site of progressive politics where transformative alternatives might be found to the current deep structural ambivalences that characterise our political horizon. The task of this book has not been to argue that sanctuary cities do or do not provide this potential. Rather it has described what the sanctuary city means to those who perform under its force, how it has been used, why, and with what effects.

Crucially, I do not foreground the contradictions in sanctuary cities to criticise sanctuary actors, but rather to clarify the complexities and tensions within which these actors operate, related to questions of borders and migration but also broader issues of exploitation, dispossession, and racialisation. While sanctuary cities are always limited, considering the increasing securitisation of nation-states it is remarkable that cities have translated any demands for more secure lives into platforms for change (some more or less successful or sustained than others). Sanctuary actors have pioneered some of the most hopeful challenges to the exclusionary logics of liberal democratic welfare states. Such states rely on flexible, precarious labour that pulls migrants into urban centres and concurrently implement cruel immigration and settlement policies that keep them on the peripheries of membership.

We must also account for the innumerable costs involved in this work, most felt by the precaritised themselves. These concerns relate to the difficulties of translating moral demands into avenues for sustainable change and the challenges of invoking a relationship of obligation, legal responsibility or imagined reciprocity that will hold elites responsible. In some cases, this relates directly to the ambiguous and shifting nature of authority itself. However, this work is essential because, as Robbie Shilliam (2018, 179) reminds us, 'it is in the micro-sites, usually coloured as "ethnic" or "immigrant", that the battles for tomorrow are first won or lost'.

As explored throughout the book, the notion of the sanctuary city provokes fundamental questions on the kinds of communities we want to create and the grounds on which we determine membership and belonging to those communities. As I write this conclusion, San Francisco has declared itself a 'Transgender Sanctuary City', remaking, once again, the meaning of the term and the values it alludes to (DeBenedetti 2024). However, the tensions that have unfolded through these chapters reveal that these declarations are not straightforward. Rather they point to sites of struggle and the deep-seated contradictions between who we think we are, what we want to become, and what we value. By elaborating on these tensions, we may work towards providing clearer answers to these fundamental questions.

Methods
Comparative Policy Ethnography

My methods involved interviews, direct and participant observations, questionnaires, field notes, content analysis, discourse analysis, oral history interviews, and archival research. I traced and mapped how and where the idea of sanctuary was taken up and how it was discussed in professional, activist or media circles, being attentive to the 'atmosphere' of situations where sanctuary was narrated (conferences, council chambers, advocate meetings, protests, NGO meetings with clients, educational events, arts events). I endeavoured to keep my approach open and flexible rather than overly prescriptive due to the diversity of assemblages in and through which sanctuary cities are constituted and to remain oriented towards the relational, fleeting, and mobile (McCann and Ward 2012).

Gathering Sanctuary Legislation and Policy Documents
I tailored my approach to each city context in order to gather relevant documents. In San Francisco, I wrote to the Clerk of the Board of Supervisors asking for all relevant legislation and policy documents relating to the 1989 City of Refuge Ordinance. I searched the Legislative Research Center which chronicles the Board of Supervisors' legislative archives and proceedings from 1998 to the present and for proceedings predating 1999 I researched the Board's Journals of Proceedings.[1] I used the search terms 'sanctuary', 'city of refuge', 'asylum', and 'undocumented'. I submitted public records requests via email under the city's 'Sunshine Ordinance' for department policies and procedures, department general orders, and training materials relating to the Sanctuary Ordinance from all 'Tier 1' organisations, departments, and agencies in the city government that most directly interact with the public and who were

specifically named in the city's Language Access Ordinance for their work with immigrant populations.[2]

In Sheffield, I submitted an FOI request for all council documents, policies, and position papers related to Sheffield's City of Sanctuary commitment and from all departments that provide services to residents.[3] I searched the local studies library for all documents related to the Sanctuary City and asylum seekers and refugees.

In Toronto, I used the search function on the municipal government website for all documents related to 'Access T.O.', 'undocumented', 'asylum', and 'sanctuary'. I also submitted a Freedom of Information request to the Toronto Municipal Clerk's office for all legislation and policy papers related to Access T.O. I submitted Freedom of Information requests via email for department policies and procedures relating to Access T.O. from departments and agencies in the city government that most directly interact with the public.[4]

In addition, in each city I submitted information requests to the municipal government for all organisations that hold tenders or contracts from the municipality to provide direct services to migrants or newcomers. I contacted all organisations listed to ask them about their sanctuary policy and, if relevant, requested an interview and to attend any meetings or trainings that were relevant to the sanctuary city policy. Moreover, in each city I collected data about eligibility and access to services at the federal, state (for California and Ontario), and city level in order to conduct interviews and understand the landscape of sanctuary at the nexus of immigration status and access to services (see Chapter 4).

Interviews and Participant Observation

While reading all academic and grey literature on sanctuary in each city I made notes of all organisations that had written reports or were mentioned as playing an important role to the making of the sanctuary city. When reviewing policy documents I noted who submitted comments, opinions, petitions, deputed at committee hearings (in San Francisco and Toronto) or were listed as members of relevant working groups or committees. I also searched for relevant organisations through strategic reports or networks in each city. I contacted all these organisations, or if the organisation had closed, I traced those mentioned to their new positions to ask for an interview. In total, I conducted 160 interviews across three cities. Interviews

Table A.1   Interviews by City and Type

	San Francisco	Sheffield	Toronto
Advocates	3	2	4
Faith-based orgs	6	2	1
Government	22	13	18
Government vendors	14	n/a	22
NGO / non-profits	13	28	12
Total	58	45	57
Combined total	160		

varied from between thirty minutes to three hours. I recorded and transcribed all the interviews myself.

In San Francisco, I contacted all organisations listed under the three main networks that help immigrants in the city (San Francisco Immigrant Legal and Education Network, the San Francisco Legal Defence Coalition, and the advocacy group Free SF[5]). In Sheffield, I contacted all organisations listed through the Strategic Regional Migration Partnership (Migration Yorkshire) and all organisations listed through Cohesion Sheffield, the strategy group that was tasked with implementing the strategic cohesion plan for the city. In Toronto, I consulted the annex of reports on Access T.O. and contacted all consulting organisations and those in the Access without Fear working group. I also contacted all Toronto members of the Ontario Coalition of Service Providers for Refugee Claimants; members of the Advisory Group of the 2019 City of Toronto Refugee Capacity Plan (EC3.5); and all members of the consultative committee for the Toronto Newcomers Strategy.[6]

I also emailed all elected municipal officers (Supervisors (SF) and Councillors (Toronto and Sheffield)). I emailed all department heads that provide direct services to residents or have direct contact with residents to ask them for an interview. In San Francisco, department heads replied that the Sanctuary Ordinance was salient to their department and many agreed to meet me for an interview. In Toronto, department heads referred me to the Newcomer Office as they considered the request out of their jurisdiction. Similarly, in Sheffield, I was referred to the Community Development Department (see below for details).

In interviews, I asked for any policy, training or document that was salient to the Sanctuary City policy (in electronic or hard copy) and also asked to attend trainings or meetings where the sanctuary city policy had relevance. In San Francisco, I was refused permission to interview anyone below the department head level at the HSA or attend trainings or meetings. The reason provided was that the City and County of San Francisco was in legal proceedings with the federal government and the head of the HSA did not want to jeopardise the case. I was able to interview the director of RISE-SF and attend trainings of social work interns for the Unified School District of San Francisco. The Office of Early Childhood and Education was extremely helpful in facilitating interviews with Family Resource Centres both in Chinatown and Mission districts. I took tours and attended classes in the Family Resource Centres. I also contacted Welcoming America and was put in touch with Chinatown YMCA. I attended training sessions for community members in sanctuary city policy.

In Sheffield, I interviewed members of the municipal government Community Development Department, and attended operational, partnership, and strategic meetings concerning refugees, migrants, and community cohesion in the municipal government. I interviewed the Public Health team, who facilitated interviews with members of the Clinical Commissioning Group and GPs, and trainings and meetings about newcomer health access. I also interviewed the Service Lead for No Recourse to Public Funds in the Children's Services Department and children's social workers. South Yorkshire Police were very cooperative with my requests for interviews. City of Sanctuary Sheffield were also very important in facilitating interviews with their own staff and partner organisations in the sector. I attended weekly drop-ins, volunteer training, helped at reception, and helped write funding applications for projects. I attended Refugee Week events, performances, and talks. SYMAAG were also crucial to my understanding of the history and current organising in Sheffield around migrants' rights. I was asked for advice on an asylum seeker needs assessment under the role of being a 'critical friend'. I also shared FOIs with organisations and attended meetings where I offered a comparative perspective on Sheffield.

In Toronto, the Newcomers Office was a key point of contact and they shared PowerPoints, training manuals, and position papers on the Access T.O. policy. Neighbourhood and Community Houses and Local Immigration

Partnerships were very important in helping me understand the networks of services in different localities in the city. No One Is Illegal Toronto were central to my understanding of the history of organising and how sanctuary emerged as a dominant frame. I attended the Network for Uninsured meetings and training for health and frontline workers in sanctuary policy. I also attended training for frontline workers with a particular focus on undocumented sex workers and the trafficking and sanctuary city nexus. I attended the Rights of Non-Status Women Network monthly meetings and helped to organise a community training and awareness raising event. I volunteered with the FCJ Refugee Centre youth group and the Roma Rights Centre. I attended community forums on workers' rights, health access, and cross-cultural understanding across the city.

By attending, organising, and participating in training and meetings, giving advice, sharing documents and FOI requests (following consent), I influenced the policy fields I was studying. However, by making my involvement explicit I hope to be as transparent as possible about the research process and how my involvement has shaped the data produced and the interpretations fixed in the writing that follows.

In addition, although not at the heart of this book on sanctuary, I also contacted religious groups to understand how the faith-based organising had developed. In San Francisco, I attended church services and interviewed volunteers who undertook accompanying work. In Sheffield, City of Sanctuary founder, Inderjit Bhoghal, is a Methodist Minister and many organisers explicitly referred to their faith. Interviews and participant observation also took place in faith-based settings. In Toronto, I attended the Southern Ontario Sanctuary Coalition.

Due to the relatively long history of 'sanctuary' in the Bay Area, I consulted four archival collections at the Graduate Theological Union in Berkeley. They included the Sanctuary Oral History Project Records, an oral history of the sanctuary movement based on interviews with religious and lay leaders in the Bay Area conducted by Eileen Purcell during 1997–1998.[7] Next, I consulted the East Bay Sanctuary Covenant Collection which includes organisational records of the Covenant from 1982 to 2000.[8] The third collection consisted of records of the National Sanctuary Defence Fund, which was an organisation established in 1984 to raise funds for the legal defence of sanctuary workers and refugees from Central America.[9] Finally, I consulted the Gustav Schultz

Sanctuary Collection (1971–72, 1981–90), which includes a wide range of sanctuary material including correspondence; working, events, and talk files; and published material.[10]. I also interviewed two key members of the movement during this time as well as listening to the oral histories collected by Eileen Purcell above.

I reviewed more than 10,000 documents in these boxes and made notes of the most relevant information. This helped me to piece together the different meanings that were given to sanctuary during this time; how sanctuary was being defined; the opposition to the sanctuary movement; and the different networks that were being built between faith-based organisations, legal and immigrant rights groups in San Francisco, and the San Francisco Government and Board of Supervisors. I also made a note of ways in which the history and key events were recorded and the way sanctuary was being narrated.

APPENDIX TWO
Table of Inland Border Controls in San Francisco, Sheffield, and Toronto

Table A.2   Inland Border Controls in San Francisco, Sheffield, and Toronto

	San Francisco	Sheffield	Toronto
Raids	Requires judicial warrant to enter building (Fourth Amendment). Rapid Response Network in operation. Regular and fully city-funded 'Know Your Rights' training in multiple languages.	Requires judicial warrant to enter building (Trespass). No 'Know Your Rights' training.	Requires judicial warrant to enter building (Trespass). Reporting to CBSA by Toronto Police. Limited capacity of 'Know Your Rights' training. Undertaken pro bono.
Police	Follows 12H of Administrative Code (Sanctuary City policy) and strong public oversight through the Police Commission. General Order 5.15 brings section 12H into SFPD Code and was last updated in January 2017. Visa status for victim or witness of crime (U and T visa) and court accompaniment policy (from District Attorney's office).	Sheffield City Council has no jurisdiction over South Yorkshire Police. SYP are partners at SCC strategic meetings. Home Office embedded officers inside South Yorkshire Police. Open collaboration between Home Office and Police. Routine checks of immigration status through racial profiling. No policy for victims or witnesses of crime.	Governed by the Ontario Police Services Act. The City of Toronto has a very limited role in shaping police policy through the TPS Board. TPS Board decided police have a duty to share immigration information with CBSA (although this is not defined in the Police Services Act or Immigration and Refugee Protection Act).

(Continued)

Table A.2   *(Continued)*

	San Francisco	Sheffield	Toronto
	Policy for victims and witnesses of crime.		Toronto Police passed a very weak 'Don't Ask' policy for Victims or Witnesses to crimes (except for 'bone fide' reasons) but they continue to call CBSA should they become aware that a victim or witness is without status. They also continue to ask the status of people charged with crimes.
Housing	Undocumented are not eligible for Public or Section 8 Housing (Section 214 of the Housing and Community Development Act). However, if one member of the family is eligible support can be provided (rent subsidy pro-rated based on number of eligible persons in household) and only that member has to have a SIN. Landlords may threaten undocumented residents with eviction/reporting to ICE in order to raise rents.	Irregular migrants for the purposes of housing are considered 'No Recourse to Public Funds'. They have no entitlement to local authority shelters or social housing. Local authorities can use discretionary power under the Care Act 2014 (section 19(1)) or Localism Act 2011 (section 1) to prevent a breach of human rights. Destitute asylum seekers in Sheffield can access ASSIST, a registered charity that provides accommodation and subsistence payments.	Precarious status residents are eligible for city run shelters but not provincially provided public housing. Toronto Shelter Services agreed an MoU with IRCC to receive federal funds to house asylum seekers regionally in the Toronto region (but outside the city). There is a firewall between this data kept at the IRCC and the CBSA (see Chapter 5).

	San Francisco	Sheffield	Toronto
		Residents may also find it difficult to privately rent as 'Right to Rent' checks were introduced by the Immigration Act 2014. Landlords may be charged with a criminal offence if they do not carry out these checks, introduced by the Immigration Act 2016.	
Health	Undocumented immigrants are not eligible for Medi-Cal, but they can receive limited emergency services such as labour and delivery care for pregnant women and limited other services. Emergency care coverage will apply to those who require medically necessary testing and healthcare related to Covid-19, even if such individuals are undocumented. HealthySF provides all residents of San Francisco a basic standard of healthcare. Some specialist services require a fee.	The UK National Health Service provides everyone with a primary doctor. Health services for precarious status migrants incur a charge. Hospitals are being encouraged to demand up-front payments. NHS does communicate with the Home Office in limited circumstances.	Ontario provides healthcare through the Ontario Health Insurance Plan (OHIP) Toronto has a network for the medically uninsured (which includes those waiting for 3 months to become eligible for services). Community Health Centres are available to those without OHIP. In light of Covid-19 Ontario expanded healthcare to all residents including those who were previously uninsured. There are no reports that hospitals report undocumented residents to CBSA.

(Continued)

Table A.2   (*Continued*)

	San Francisco	Sheffield	Toronto
Education	Every child who lives in California has the right to a free public education regardless of immigration status. Non-citizen parents can also vote in School Board elections from 2018. All California public colleges and universities and many other private colleges and universities admit undocumented students. Undocumented students cannot receive federal financial aid. AB 540 allows students to apply for in-state tuition at California public colleges. The California Dream Act of 2011 permits those who qualify for AB 540 to also qualify for some types of state financial aid.	The UK Education Act requires all children between 5 and 18 years old to attend school. Schools collect nationality and country of birth information but this is not currently shared with the Home Office. Providing the nationality or country of birth of children to the school is optional. Other personal information collected through the school census (home address for example) is stored in the National Pupil Database. Parents have to complete the school census. This information can be shared with the Home Office. Ineligibility for domestic tuition rates, and the inaccessibility of financial aid all present significant barriers to access to post-secondary education for undocumented people.	The Ontario Education Act requires all Ontario residents aged between 6 and 18 years old to attend school. Tuition fees are charged to tourists and visitors. Fears of reporting, ineligibility for domestic tuition rates, and the inaccessibility of financial aid all present significant barriers to access to post-secondary education for undocumented people in Ontario.

	San Francisco	Sheffield	Toronto
Welfare	No City or County employee will ask for migration status (12H of Administrative Code). Precarious status residents are not eligible for income support provided through the state (CAL-Works, CAL-Fresh, CAAP Cash Assistance). They are eligible for child care but in practice free places are oversubscribed.	Precarious status migrants are not eligible for national income support. Some assistance may be provided for families with children if the local authority undertakes a Human Rights Assessment. In Sheffield, this is also accompanied by reporting the family to the Home Office.	The Ontario Works Act asks for immigration status. This information can be disclosed to CBSA for the purpose of enforcing the IRPA.
Child services	Children and families are not reported to ICE from Child Protective Services. One case of chain reporting to ICE (see Mancina 2016). There are no age assessments for unaccompanied minors.	Children's services in Sheffield routinely report undocumented families to the Home Office.	Governed by the Ontario Association of Children's Aid Societies (OACAS). Reports that OACAS inform police when dealing with child abuse, resulting in charges and/or reporting to CBSA. Best interests of the child interpreted as children deported with mother (unless court order grants custody to another).

Notes

Introduction

1. On 25 January 2017 within five days of Donald Trump's inauguration as President he issued 'Enhancing Public Safety in the Interior of the United States (EO 13768)', which was swiftly followed by a Department of Homeland Security (DHS) memorandum, 'Enforcement of the Immigration Laws to Serve the National Interest'. The Executive Order specifically targets 'sanctuary jurisdictions'. In Section 9, it states 'jurisdictions that wilfully refuse to comply with 8 U.S.C. 1373 [addressing information-sharing regarding immigration and citizenship status between government agencies and the Immigration and Naturalization Service] are not eligible to receive federal grants, except as deemed necessary for law enforcement purposes.' In response, on 31 January the City and County of San Francisco filed in the US District Court (Northern District of California) asking the court to declare Section 9(a) unconstitutional. Following almost two years of legal proceedings the Ninth Circuit ruled that the federal government could not withhold the grants; however, it added that this ruling did not extend nationally. Three other regional federal appeals court have ruled against the administration, but New York's Second Circuit allowed it to go forward and declined to reconsider its ruling.

2. There is some debate regarding whether San Francisco was the first city to self-define in the USA but it was among the first, and the first to incorporate this designation into municipal governance as the 'City of Refuge' Ordinance first in 1985 and in a strengthened ordinance in 1989.

3. My previous research had focused on how frontline workers seemed to be making up migration policy through their everyday decisions. I found from long-term ethnographic fieldwork with new migrant families who came to be known as 'Romanian Roma' that decisions about their legal residency and migration status often depended on the discretionary decisions of child welfare workers. I became increasingly interested in the occupational identity of these frontline workers and the dilemmas they experienced as they effectively 'made-up' migration and settlement policy on the fly. At the same time, I became aware of work done by Graham Hudson about the discretionary decisions of frontline workers in the sanctuary city of Toronto and how their decisions could affect whether a migrant was provided with access to services or

reported to the immigration authorities. I began to wonder what might affect front-line workers' decisions and whether sanctuary cities effectively provided a way to contest migration policy from the ground up. I decided that an interesting entry point would be to look at sanctuary cities across different national frameworks. I chose a pioneering city in the three countries that had actively taken up the notion of the 'sanctuary city' and included this designation in their municipal government policies. It is not a coincidence, but rooted in deep historical underpinnings as shown by Chapter 3, that these countries utilise the notion of the sanctuary city.

4. Studying through calls for charting how power creates webs and relations between actors, institutions, and discourses across time and space (Shore and Wright 1997, 11). The concrete method for 'following a policy' means 'tracing policy-relevant actors, objects, acts and language to tease out connections and observing how policies bring together individuals, discourses and institutions and the new kinds of networks, relations and subjects this process creates' (Wright and Reinhold 2011, 102).

5. California's gross domestic product (GDP) in 2022 was $3.6 trillion representing 14.3% of the total US economy. This is larger than both the UK ($2.67 trillion) and Canada ($1.64 trillion).

6. Informed by these processes of dispossession, I use the term 'precaritised residents' in this book rather than un(der)documented migrants. This term alludes to the blurred boundaries and contested nature of defining the people that sanctuary cities are aimed to support. Migration scholars have long argued that migrant statuses are fluid; not only do individuals repeatedly move between 'legality' and 'illegality' (Calavita 2003, Kubal 2013; Anderson and Ruhs 2010), but also underlying legal categories and potential paths into and out of irregularity change over time (Cvajner and Sciortino 2010; Düvell 2011). I also use this term to allude to the longer historical complexities of exploitation, deprivation, and racialisation that will be explored further in Chapter 2.

7. Between 2010 and 2015 there was a 54.7% increase in evictions, the majority of which were in the Mission District, the historically Latinx area (San Francisco Anti-Displacement Coalition 2016; San Francisco Rent Board 2016). Eviction-induced displacement is not only a loss of home (including identity; memory; structures of feeling; space; scales and intensities of affiliation; and materiality), but contributes to widening urban inequalities, the reproduction of poverty (Desmond 2012), and is also a political loss. Due to the spiralling rental costs in the Bay Area, those evicted move far beyond the bounds of the city (Walker and Schafran 2015) with particular consequences for those with precarious legal status who lose social and political rights and the hard won (albeit limited) protections that many of them fought for.

8. In addition, the recent rebranding of the Mission District and Latinx culture as a commodity to be consumed can be seen as an iteration of 'racial capitalism' defined as 'the development, organisation and expansion of capitalist society which has pursued essentially racial directions' (Robinson 1983, 2). The gentrification of the Mission 'preys upon' and actively commodifies Mission Latinx culture to boost property value. As McElroy states, 'the gentrification is premised upon tech speculation or

practices in which future real estate value is linked to the desires of those imbricated in techno-capitalist economies' (2019, 827).

9. There are historical continuations between the wholesale purges of African Americans in the SoMa and Fillmore district (Rothstein 2017) and Filipinx in Manilatown (Habal 2007) in the 1960s and 1970s and the current piecemeal 'silent sorting' of residents in the Mission (Marcuse 2015).

10. Defined as those who either voluntarily or through their employment enact sanctuary policy or perform under its force.

11. United States Census Bureau 'Foreign born residents in San Francisco' Available at: https://www.census.gov/quickfacts/fact/table/sanfranciscocountycalifornia/ PST045222 accessed 30 November 2023.

12. Migration Policy Institute. 2019. 'Profile of the Unauthorized Population: San Francisco County, CA'. Available at: https://www.migrationpolicy.org/data/ unauthorized-immigrant-population/county/6075 accessed 15 November 2023.

13. See Sheffield City Council 'Population in Sheffield' 2021 output release https:// www.sheffield.gov.uk/your-city-council/population-in-sheffield accessed 14 November 2023.

14. City Population Mapper Burngreave. Available at: https://www.citypopulation .de/en/uk/yorkshireandthehumber/wards/sheffield/E05010861__burngreave/ accessed 14 November 2023.

15. The Greater Toronto Area includes six local boroughs—Etobicoke, North York, Scarborough, York, East York, and the City of Toronto plus the cities of Mississauga and Brampton.

16. In addition there is general confusion regarding which services are run by the City (and therefore under the jurisdiction of Access T.O.) and those run by other agencies who could freely report an undocumented resident. See Chapter 3 for further details.

17. Post-colonial scholars argue that much previous analysis has used ideas of class, poverty, social marginalisation, and stigmatisation without fully accounting for how cities act, 'as a mechanism through which capital produces race as a socio-political category of distinction and discrimination in the first place and as a form of structural coercion that is built into capitalist structures and institutions, rather than a discrete act that may be spatially expressed' (Danewid 2020, 296). These scholars see race as a socio-spatial relation that is 'both constitutive of the city and produced by it' (Pulido 2000, 12). In this reading, global cities are seen as mechanisms through which capital produces raced space (Gilmore 2007).

18. As Cedric Robinson's (1983) *Black Marxism* reminds us, this is not surprising: capitalism has historically operated through racial projects that differentiate between those associated with rights, wages, and citizenship and those subject to super-exploitation and dispossession. Racial capitalism denotes, according to Bhattacharyya (2018, 5), 'a process by which capitalist formations create by default the edge-populations that serve as the other and limit of the working class'. Shilliam similarly shows

how processes of racialisation in Western societies have long operated through the shifting categorisation between 'the deserving and undeserving poor through ever more expansive terms that have incorporated working classes, colonial "natives" and nationalities' (2018, 6).

19. The post-war period's massive urban renewal and public housing programmes drew on urban planning rationales developed through colonial governance, including techniques of slum clearance and racial segregation which were framed as a question of public health. Disease, criminality, alcoholism, prostitution, and other 'dangers' might 'pollute' the white body politic.

20. I agree with Doreen Massey (1993) regarding the terminology of the 'global city'. She remarks that the global cities phenomenon also follows distinctive patterns of spatial change. However, she contends it is not necessarily the globalisation of cities such as London, Paris, New York, and Tokyo that has caused shifts in investment and population, but rather their adherence to policies of deregulation. Arguing that the economies of global cities are far more diverse than are often acknowledged, she states that the global cities hypothesis itself is a way of naturalising policy choices as a result of inevitable market forces, and also valorising the most competitive and profitable part of a city's economy by having those represent the entire city. In other words, our analytical paradigms for describing global cities are not neutral; they play a role in encouraging these market-orientated developments. It is for this reason that I choose the term 'globalised city' to indicate the political and processual nature of the term.

21. In liberal theory, citizenship is theorised as universal, meaning that all members of the political community are granted equal rights. In the ideal, there are no partial citizens. This notion of citizenship has now been successfully challenged, spearheaded by Iris Marion Young (1989).

22. In addition to formal, juridical citizenship, citizenship also concerns moral and performative dimensions of membership, which define meanings and practices of belonging in society (Staeheli 1997). Scholarly work highlights the possibility of irregular migrants being included in some spheres or aspects of social life but simultaneously excluded from many others (Castles and Davidson 2000; Cvajner and Sciortino 2010; Mezzadra and Neilson 2012; Anderson and Ruhs 2010; Chauvin and Garcés-Mascareñas 2012). The notion of citizenship has been further nuanced through ideas of conditionality or continuously probationary citizenship (Anderson 2013; Watters 2007). State practices of revoking citizenship reveal how citizenship, while claiming equality, has always been a privilege based along class, gender, and racialised axes of difference (Kapoor 2018). Moreover, citizenship does not only confer rights on privileged categories but is embedded in the creation, definition and manipulation of those categories of identity. As Isin extensively explores, 'the theories that define citizenship as a space of privilege neglect that it requires the constitution of these others to become possible' (2002, 4). Precaritised residents are integral to the meaning of citizenship. Citizenship is not merely a status or institution but a relationship (Isin and Ruppert 2015).

Chapter 1

1. It draws inspiration from methodological innovations from interpretive social science (Geertz 1973). The method details how we can 'follow sanctuary policy' (Marcus 1995), in a 'policy field' (Shore and Wright 1997), to 'study though' each sanctuary city (Wright and Reinhold 2011). The outcome of this method is tracing cities' 'history of the present' (see Humphris 2020a, 2020b and 2021), struggles over sanctuary meanings (including meanings from various 'elsewheres' (McCann and Ward 2012)), how governing discourses become institutionalised and politics is rendered technical (Murray Li 2007), and how sanctuary policy can both further and disrupt the interests of capital and the neoliberalised subject (Clarke et al. 2015).

2. My approach to comparison focuses on relationality drawing inspiration from anthropologist Frederick Barth. In his Sidney Mintz Lecture, Barth (2002) proposed the project of 'comparative ethnography'. Barth focuses on knowledge. Instead of providing a rigid definition of knowledge, he shifts his attention to the mechanisms that surround this wide conceptual space such as validation of knowledge, trajectories of the changing corpus of knowledge, and mechanisms to keep knowledge coherent. This move enables Barth to make comparisons among societies with respect to knowledge while simultaneously paying attention to particular mechanisms that shape knowledge and modify the understanding of knowledge itself.

3. The ethnographic text must be seen as only one perspective, a reflection on the events that were experienced. In the words of Appadurai, 'the ethnographic text is the more or less creative imposition of order on the many conversations that lie at the heart of fieldwork' (1988, 16). This book is therefore a narrative which gives reality a possible shape, with this perspective that is focused solely on data production (rather than data gathering).

4. City and County of San Francisco Board of Supervisors Ordinance Number 190009. Available at City and County of San Francisco—File #: 190009 (legistar.com) accessed 19 January 2022.

5. David Mosse's anthropology of development details the labour needed to stabilise policy meanings (Mosse 2004). The common theoretical reference point for critical policy studies, policy geography, and anthropology of development is actor-network-theory drawn from Latour's sociological approach. All three literatures talk about policies being 'actants', which have agency and change as they enter into relations with other actors, objects, and institutions. The idea that translation is crucial to help understand the social production of meaning and the making of social worlds is drawn from Latour's work on how scientists continually construct and manage the social contexts of which they form a part through a diverse range of elements.

6. Shore, Wright and Pero state that policies must be studied through how they are enacted and develop through everyday practice (Shore et al. 2011, 21). In Anglo-American urban studies this shift to empirical practice-oriented research was provoked by critical approaches to 'the urban' which questioned the urban as a coherent site

of analysis. Reflecting a wider intellectual current that argues for a relational under-standing of space (Allen and Cochrane 2007; Massey 1993), critical studies of urban policy have recently begun to open up, or 'unbound', the urban as a coherent geo-graphical site.

7. This insight is based on a crucial development in anthropology of policy that can be charted between Shore and Wright's first book (1997) and their second book co-authored with Davide Pero (2011). They respond to critiques of 'ideological decon-structivism' that fails to acknowledge the relationship between rhetoric, 'mobilizing simplifications of policy and politics' and the world as understood and experienced within the lives of policy actors (see Mosse 2004, 644). The 2011 edited volume in-cludes interactions between ideas and relationships and therefore remains attentive to the complexity of policy and institutional practice; the social life of projects, or-ganisations, and professionals; the diversity of interests behind policy models and the perspective of actors themselves.

Chapter 2

1. Before embarking on this historical chapter, I offer a word of caution in line with Engin Isin who argues that the aim of undertaking the task of appropriating history in broad sequences is not to find 'solutions' to 'problems' but rather to question the limits within which we think about those problems, invoking different histories and formulating new sets of questions.

2. The silence on colonial legacies is not confined to sanctuary city scholarship but reverberates more broadly through contemporary urban scholarship. It is indic-ative of a wider set of racial erasures evident in foundational scholarship on urban-ism, which grounded the discipline and thought in Orientalist stances. For example, Weber's The City (non-legitimate domination) (1958 [1922]). Contemporary scholars have challenged Weber's central thesis that the self-organisation of urban citizens as emerged in medieval Europe helped explain why Europe has dominated the world for the past five hundred years (Isin 2002: 189). As Picker describes, 'comparative so-ciology argues that medieval Central and Northern European cities were the first real examples of modern democratic citizenship, essentially due to the coeval emergence of guilds and other non-kin groups that represented a rupture in previous kin-based citizenry. The main condition for these autonomous groups to appear was the simul-taneous presence of Christianity and capitalism, which suggest that only in the Oc-cident does the city exist in the specific sense of the word' (2019, 7). The constructed asymmetry between Orient and Occident, the latter being seen as the only place that the city truly exists and therefore superior, was both the process and the product of colonialism. New histories show urban citizenship was not unique to Europe and did not deliver what Weber claimed (Prak 2018, 4).

3. Following Cedric Robinson (1983), I acknowledge that renderings of class, race, and gender to subjugate and persecute ascribed groups did not begin with colonial encounters but took on new forms through imperial governance.

4. I want to note that racialisation is not static and different characteristics or group identities can move into or out of negative racialisation. This is made clear through Hirota's detailed examination of how Irish immigrants were targeted until they migrated out of that racialised category and became 'white' (Hirota 2016).

5. I am also attentive to how different colonial projects unfolded differently, and that 'the quality and intensity of racism vary enormously in different colonial contexts and at different historical moments in any particular colonial encounter' (Stoler 1989, 137–138). The circulations between colony and metropole should therefore be seen as complex and diversified and relations that need to be explored rather than assumed to take on any particular character.

6. By the seventeenth century, Spanish and Dutch settlements had distinct intentions to transplant the metropoles' political and spatial order. Britain and France were slow to assemble such strategies and were content to allow colonists to articulate their identities and follow local and contingent circumstances to establish settlements. However, once Britain and France were dedicated to permanent settlement in North America from the middle of the seventeenth century, these strategies shifted and Britain in particular established sophisticated technologies of government (more so than the Spanish and Dutch) (Isin 2002, 180).

7. The advantages of population density in towns were three-fold for colonial administrations. First, they afforded convenient access to labour when needed, second, administration of justice was less costly, and third, administration of health was more efficient. In short, land settlement was associated with efficient administration of the population to be conducive to the wealth and strength of the colony. British colonial governance also implemented a particular spatial order as towns were laid out corresponding to social divisions of the population according to status (Isin 2002, 182ff.). There are distinct histories for each city, but the growth of towns heralded two general consequences. First, health and sanitation of the poor became a concern for government. Second, citizenship practices challenged loyalty to distant governors. It should be noted in seventeenth century New England towns and their local institutions became the prime political institutions of provincial society, and not provinces or states (Zuckerman 1970, 19, 24, 46–47). Isin argues rebellious sentiments in newly formed towns led to the formation of municipal corporations.

8. There were three forms of city colony during this period: chartered colonies, proprietary colonies, and royal colonies (see Isin 1992, 69–90 for overview).

9. After the American Revolution, British governing elites in 'close corporations' were seen as vestiges of British power which led to the doctrine of state supremacy over cities (Frug 1980, 1109; Teaford 1975, 51). The legacy of colonial towns that were not so tightly governed in 'close corporations' gave rise to two legal principles: right to local self-government and municipal home rule, which some US cities still uphold.

10. The development of citizenship practices in corporate colonies in America were considered to have caused the rebellion of the thirteen colonies (Isin 1999, 99) and the fear of rebellion changed the shape of governing cities in Upper and Lower

Canada (for details see Isin 1999, 99–131). One of the largest early influxes of refugees to what is now Canada were loyalists from the thirteen colonies (Kelley and Trebilcock 2000: 38).

11. For the debates concerning the incorporation of Toronto, see Isin 1999, 145–149.

12. These practices continued well after the American Revolution and were the spine of westward expansion of the new United States (Lange 2006: 1443). San Francisco was established in 1776 by Spanish colonists (Saunt 2014, 81). Despite differences between Spanish and English systems of colonial governance (Prak 2018, 282), when California entered the Union in 1850, it implemented many policies and practices towards the itinerant poor that had been developed from the Atlantic coastal states.

13. There is a large and artful scholarship on histories and legacies of colonial administration on how the city creates raced space. This literature is drawn upon in Chapter 1 and further discussion on configurations and articulations of racialised urban space is not possible within the economy of this chapter. However, for important work on how urban space becomes a medium for racism see Cross and Keith (1993); Legg and McFarlane (2008); Low (1996); Nightingale (2012); and Picker et al. (2019). For how colonial cities and peripheries have historically functioned as 'social laboratories' where new security strategies designed to 'pacify' urban geographies could be tested before they were shipped back to the metropole see Barder (2015); Shilliam (2018); and Sinclair and Williams (2007). For the links between urban planning and social hygiene see Worpole (2000).

14. As Baseler notes, 'when the native Irish proved intractable, England embarked on a massive program of removal replacement. . . When similar problems emerged in America, the same devices of removal and transplantation were adopted' (1998, 35). Legal principles of deportation and containment circulated between Britain and its colonies in Ireland and on the Atlantic coast in a shared Anglophone moral universe (Hirota 2017, 187; Baseler 1998, 25–27, 161–162).

15. The eighteenth century saw all possibilities for free African Americans to participate in citizenship practices and Indigenous Americans to have some sovereignty over their own land completely disappear (Prak 2017, 294). Citizenship became an exclusively 'whites-only' institution in the colonies during this time.

16. In the seventeenth century there were some possibilities for freed African Americans to participate in citizenship practices, such as being recruited in the militias that helped to defend the newly conquered territories from the Indigenous populations they had expelled from the land. These trained bands at first recruited indiscriminately but later different territories excluded freed slaves and indentured servants. In South Carolina, the turning point came in 1739 when a large slave revolt was put down with great effort. From then on, militias became exclusively white organisations. By the middle of the eighteenth century, openings for urban citizenship had disappeared for 'Indians, free blacks, mulattos, white servants and apprentices and those without a fixed abode' (Prak 2018, 292). By the start of the American Revolution, citizenship was a whites-only institution in the United States.

17. Poor laws were evident in New England and the South (including Connecticut, Rhode Island, Pennsylvania, Delaware, and Virginia) beginning in 1683. They authorised local officials to send transient beggars to other colonies or to 'the country from whence they came' (Hirota 2017, 43).

18. The early discussion of tax-financed social assistance based on the poor law tradition throughout the British Empire pushed the colonies toward tax-financed social protection, an institutional legacy that carried into contemporary times.

19. State poor laws restricted public assistance to individuals with a 'settlement'— typically, residence in a community for a period of months or a few years. Under this logic, neighbours (whether citizens or not) were entitled to support in time of need; transients were not. It wasn't until the 1970s, however, that welfare became limited by the terms under which an individual entered the nation. Through this move, national citizenship eclipsed state and local citizenship as a key boundary of social citizenship (see Fox 2016).

20. By 1824 New York City stopped the deportation of paupers and legislated that those with residence should be supported in alms-houses (Law 2014, 114).

21. Key legislation throughout the early nineteenth century includes the Royal Commission on Education of the 'Lower Orders' 1818; the Poor Law Amendment Act 1834; the 1840 Report of the Select Committee on the Health of Towns and the Sanitary Conditions of the Labouring Population (1842) (Isin 1992, 50–55 and Kelley and Trebilcock 2000, 46–51).

22. These notions may have been fuelled by forced removal policies such as the Transportation Act 1717, which banished convicts to colonies (Kanstroom 2007, 41; Baseler 1998, 5).

23. For an overview of California's incorporation into the Union see Smith 2013, 7–9. For a review of the relationship between population, territory, and wealth in California from the Gold Rush in 1848 see Smith 2013, 21–46 including migrations from the United States, Mexico, Chile, Peru, China, and Hawai'i, each bringing regional and temporally distinct forms of wage labour, slavery, contract labour, debt bondage, peonage, and indentured servitude.

24. The Chinese Exclusion cases and specifically *Fong Yue Ting* were founded in the plenary power doctrine that had been established in the justification for expelling Indigenous people from their land (see Kanstroom 2007, 64–67, 95–107). The dilemma posed by Indigenous sovereignty related to the source of federal power. This dilemma was resolved through the notion of 'inherent power' through the 'Doctrine of Discovery', which gave the federal government 'ultimate title' over Indigenous land. This inherent power was also used to invalidate San Francisco ordinances designed to drive Chinese laundries out of business (see Kanstroom 2007, 72–73).

25. It should also be noted that there were particular gendered effects with woman also being targeted (see Smith 2013, 141ff.).

26. Before 1875, California permitted state commissioners, at their discretion, to exact a bond for certain arriving immigrants. In Chy Lung v. Freeman, 92 U.S. 275, 277

(1875), the Supreme Court established the notion of federal exclusivity in the field of immigration.

27. Notable initiatives include the Sheffield Society for Constitutional Information inspired by Thomas Paine (1791); the Sheffield Political Union for universal suffrage (1830); Trade Unions (from 1824) and anti-slavery movements (from 1825).

28. Only 3,504 were eligible to vote from a population in 1831 of 91,000. Eligibility was restricted to adult males with a property worth more than £10 per annum.

29. From 1747, the Cutlers' Company actively began encouraging 'foreigners' (defined as anyone residing outside Hallamshire) to Sheffield through newspaper advertisements. Workmen were recruited from London, Birmingham, York, and Newcastle, causing resentment from the locally based workforce who called on the Company to protect them through tighter regulation of entry into their occupations. Local workers lost their battle in 1814 when Parliament removed all legal powers of regulation from the Cutlers' Company.

30. The relationship between states and federal governments over who had ultimate authority for determining the relation between population and territory was being fought out in the domain of Fugitive Slave Laws that inscribed that the power to legislate on matters involving fugitive slaves was exclusive to national government but states were not bound to enforce that law through their own judicial systems (Baker 2012).

31. It is important to note that in many cases these statutes aimed to deter the poor irrespective of their national identity. They also applied to US citizens coming from other states (Neuman 1996).

32. Fox artfully explores how the consequences of decentralised social assistance policy-making were not the same for all disadvantaged groups and the importance of local context with gendered effects in the US context. In particular, she details the crucial role of social workers who could be powerful allies (particularly for southern and eastern European immigrants) or tireless opponents (when they identified their clients as African American or Mexican) (Fox 2012, 15).

33. Also evident across the three countries are the actions of relief providers who did sometimes use citizenship, legal status or the perception that one was a foreigner to justify expelling those who requested relief based on racialised assumptions, indicating the gap between policy and practice is longstanding (Fox 2012; Damer 2000; Ravetz 2003; Frost 2011).

Chapter 3

1. This is important because ICE operates from county jails and therefore the county sheriff is crucial in the prison-to-deportation pipeline (see Avila and Tosh 2024).

2. See Introduction, note 1 for details.

3. Before 1875, California permitted state commissioners, at their discretion, to exact a bond for certain arriving immigrants. In Chy Lung v. Freeman, 92 U.S. 275, 277

(1875), the Supreme Court established the notion of federal exclusivity in the field of immigration.

4. See Huyen Pham, *The Inherent Flaws in the Inherent Authority Position: Why Inviting Local Enforcement of Immigration Laws Violates the Constitution*, 31 Fla. St. U. L. Rev. 965 (2004), 970–71, 975–76; Cristina M. Rodríguez, *The Significance of the Local in Immigration Regulation*, 106 Mich. L. Rev. 567 (2008), 581–90; Rick Su, *A Localist Reading of Local Immigration Regulation*, 86 N.C. L. Rev. 1619 (2008).

5. See, e.g., *Understanding 'Sanctuary Cities,'* 59 B.C. L. Rev. 1703, 1741–43 (Lasch et al. 2018) for discussion of the 'constitutional safeguards for administrative arrest warrants' in the immigration context; David S. Rubenstein and Pratheepan Gulasekaram, *Immigration Exceptionalism*, 111 Nw. U. L. Rev. 583, 645 (2017).

6. The rationale of local control is not without its downsides. The 'states' rights' frame has historically been associated with conservative recalcitrance to federal reform efforts, including in the civil rights arena. With respect to the treatment of immigrants, local autonomy is sometimes deployed in defence of anti-immigrant measures. Nevertheless, such assertions of local control are frequently bounded by equality principles acting either directly through the Equal Protection Clause or indirectly through the doctrine of pre-emption. See, e.g., Guttentag (2013) arguing that 'immigrant equality is an essential-and forgotten ingredient in contemporary Supremacy Clause analysis'; and Motomura (2010) who describes how anti-discrimination arguments on behalf of undocumented immigrants tend to be obliquely asserted through institutional competence claims like pre-emption.

7. Cities and Local Government Devolution Act (2016). Available at: https://www .legislation.gov.uk/ukpga/2016/1/contents/enacted accessed 17 January 2022.

8. See Liberty's *Care don't Share* report for the extent of the entwinement of immigration control in UK service delivery (Bradley 2018).

9. The local authorities were: Liverpool, Oxford, Brent, Croydon, Enfield, Islington, Hackney, Haringey, Lambeth, Newham, and Rugby. This was in response to a report that the Greater London Authority shared data with the Home Office about non-UK rough sleepers to facilitate immigration control. Agreement obtained through the Freedom of Information Act (FOIA) by Liberty and reported on by Townsend (2017). See also Mohdin (2019).

10. For the long history of Toronto and British Canadian Cities see the fine-grained account in Engin Isin's (1992) book *Cities without Citizens* particularly Chapter 2 which explains and develops the typology of the autonomous city, the early modern city and the modern city.

11. Armenta argues that there is a paucity of research on immigration and policing but this scholarship is now growing. See Armenta (2017) and Maynard (2017).

12. See Obama's 2011 'sensitive locations' memo, U.S. Immigration and Customs Enforcement "Enforcement Actions at or Focused on Sensitive Locations." October 24, 2011, Policy Number 10029.2. Available at: https://www.ice.gov/doclib/ero-outreach/ pdf/10029.2-policy.pdf accessed on 17 January 2022. This policy was reintroduced

with more detail of 'protected areas' by Biden in 2021: U.S. Department of Homeland Security, "Guidelines for Enforcement Actions in or Near Protected Areas." October 27, 2021. Available at: https://www.dhs.gov/sites/default/files/publications/21_1027 _opa_guidelines-enforcement-actions-in-near-protected-areas.pdf accessed 17 January 2022.

13. For in-depth detail on the history and evolution of San Francisco's immigrant rights advocacy and sanctuary organising see Mancina (2016) and Humphris (2021).

14. Alongside access to services listed here immigration enforcement has also been diffused to other areas of everyday life. For example, in the UK, since 30 October 2017, banks and building societies have had to do immigration checks on all customers every three months and are required to report to the Home Office. In addition, the UK Driving and Vehicle Licensing Agency (DVLA) is only allowed to issue a driving licence to 'lawful residents' in the UK. The DVLA can also revoke a driving licence and does not have to notify the licence holder (Independent Chief Inspector of Borders and Immigration 2016). In California, Governor Brown signed AB 60 into law in 2013, which directs the Department of Motor Vehicles (DMV) to issue a driver's license to any California resident who is eligible, regardless of immigration status. However, the DMV database is shared with ICE and therefore can be used to funnel residents into the deportation pipeline (National Immigration Law Center 2018).

15. San Francisco Police Department (1995) General Order 5.15 Enforcement of Immigration Laws 13 December 1995. Available at: https://www.sanfranciscopolice.org/ sites/default/files/FileCenter/Documents/14776-DGO5.15.pdf accessed 17 January 2022.

16. San Francisco Police Department (2017) General Order 5.15 Enforcement of Immigration Laws Update Packet #57 14 July 2017. Available at: https://www .sanfranciscopolice.org/sites/default/files/2018-11/A%2017-163%20Department %20General%20Order%205.15%20Enforcement%20of%20Immigration%20Laws %20Update%20Packet%2057.pdf accessed 17 January 2022.

17. Group names correspond to police records.

18. There is a state form called the MC13 which requires the applicant's name and other basic demographic information (age and identifying gender). There are 17 PRUCOL categories. Applicants declare under penalty of perjury which category of PRUCOL they fall into when they sign the form. San Francisco Human Servies Agency keeps the form on file and there is no further process to confirm eligibility for services.

19. In San Francisco the immigrants' rights community came together to start the Undocufund to support families affected by the pandemic who were not eligible for federal or state support https://www.undocufund-sf.org/en/

20. Access to health for undocumented residents in cities, 19 November 2020. https://www.youtube.com/watch?v=IlIA4TVKIVg&feature=youtu.be

21. In Toronto, non-citizens' access to care is shaped by four factors according to Landolt (2022): the complex regulatory matrix of medical insurance and immigration policy, networks that advocate to extend access, cultural narratives of deservingness and membership, and the deployment of discretion (see also Villegas 2013).

22. Midwifery services are not tied to health insurance in Ontario. Any pregnant woman can be referred to a midwife for care through the Canadian Prenatal Nutrition Programme; however, if the woman has a high-risk pregnancy, she may need to see an obstetrician. While I was conducting fieldwork in Toronto, an issue was emerging where hospitals were not issuing newborns of undocumented mothers with health cards. The 'Network for Uninsured' reported that, increasingly, the regulations were being interpreted in a different way and the cards were not being routinely issued unless advocated for.

23. San Francisco Unified School District RISE-SF: Refugee and Immigrant Supports in Education. Available at: https://www.sfusd.edu/services/student-supports -programs/refugee-immigrant-supports-education accessed 17 January 2022.

24. San Francisco Department of Elections Non-Citizen Registration and Voting. https://sfelections.sfgov.org/non-citizen-registration-and-voting See also: San Francisco Municipal Elections Code Ordinance Number 206–21 Non-United States Citizen Voting in School Board Elections File Number 210961, 18 October 2021. Available at https://sfbos.org/sites/default/files/o0206-21.pdf accessed 17 January 2022.

25. Education Act, RSO 1990, c E.2. Available at: https://canlii.ca/t/556js accessed 17 January 2022.

26. Immigration and Refugee Protection Act, SC 2001, c 27. Available at: https:// canlii.ca/t/556xz accessed 17 January 2022

27. Education Act, RSO 1990, s 49(6). Available at: https://canlii.ca/t/556js accessed 17 January 2022.

28. Education Act, RSO 1990, s 49(7)(c)(iii). Available at: https://canlii.ca/t/556js accessed 17 January 2022.

29. Education Act, RSO 1990, s 49(7)(e)(ii). Available at: https://canlii.ca/t/556js accessed 17 January 2022.

30. Education Act, RSO 1990, s 49(7)(e)(i). Available at: https://canlii.ca/t/556js accessed 17 January 2022.

31. In the UK, Schedule 2, Part 1, paragraph 4 of the Data Protection Act allows data processors to set aside a person's data protection rights under the EU General Data Protection Regulation where fulfilling those rights would prejudice 'the maintenance of effective immigration control' or the 'the investigation or detection of activities that would undermine the maintenance of effective immigration control' (Data Protection Act 2018, Schedule 2, paragraph 4(1)(a) Available at: http://www.legislation.gov.uk/ ukpga/2018/12/schedule/2/paragraph/4/enacted accessed 17 January 2022). As mentioned in the Introduction, the UK Government has contracted a private sector organisation to build an immigrant status checking database that can be accessed by the government alongside private companies, landlords, banks, employers, and all other agencies that are being bestowed immigration duties; see Proc539 Status Checking Project Development Partner. Available at: https://www.digitalmarketplace.service .gov.uk/digital-outcomes-and-specialists/opportunities/12770 accessed 24 November 2020. See also: Independent Chief Inspector of Borders and Immigration (2018).

32. Canada has strict privacy laws. Under the Municipal Freedom of Information and Protection of Privacy Act (MFIPPA), the City cannot disclose personal information to another government except in two very limited circumstances: Law enforcement investigations and through a statutory requirement (for example Canada Revenue Agency for tax audit purposes or Ministry of Labour for health and safety purposes). There was an MoU between Toronto Social Services and CBSA but it was scrapped in 2017. Freedom of Information requests detailed that there was no formal MoU between TPS and CBSA but ad hoc collaboration continues (see above).

33. At the EU level there has been an increase in using people's personal data to criminalise migrants. The interoperability framework connects four different databases, namely, the Schengen Information System (SIS), visa applications from outside the EU to come to the EU (VIS), asylum applications within the EU (Eurodac), and the database that deals with EU foreign nationals with criminal convictions (ECRIS). These databases now speak to each other (see Jones 2019). The entwining of data technologies and border controls has been highlighted by researchers across Europe (see Molnar 2020).

34. See Cybelle Fox (2016, 1055) for the history of confidentiality in the Social Security Board.

35. 'Anti-deportation and anti-detention', Sanctuary: What's Next Conference, 12 November 2020. Available at: https://www.youtube.com/watch?v=GsrCgrg74jE &feature=emb_err_woyt accessed 17 January 2022.

Chapter 4

1. Benedict Anderson's foundational text explained how the boundedness of the state meant that its component objects were countable, and hence able to be incorporated into state organisation (Anderson 1991, 184). James Scott built on this idea to argue that 'state simplifications' such as naming populations and then counting them 'are like maps that are not intended to successfully represent the actual activity of the society they depict but to represent only that slice of it that is of interest for the official observer' (Scott 1998, 3).

2. For example, in 2000, the San Francisco Mayor's office estimated the city missed 100,000 people resulting in $300 million lost in federal revenue over the next decade.

3. Since the fieldwork for this research ceased Toronto has launched a 'Toronto for All' campaign for 'undocumented residents' following recognition of the frontline work that many undocumented residents continued to do through the Covid-19 pandemic. https://www.toronto.ca/community-people/get-involved/community/toronto -for-all/undocumented-residents/

4. A city vendor is a non-governmental organisation that is contracted by the municipal government to carry out a service.

5. For example, see the Change.org petition 'Keep Victor Mujakachi safe'. Available at: https://www.change.org/p/home-office-keep-victor-mujakachi-safe accessed 20 January 2022.

6. Abolitionism is a term associated with protest on grounds of inhumanity and originated in the calls to abolish slavery. Recently it extended to the abolition of prisons and has been taken up within wider critical academic perspectives. The abolitionist stance rejects reformism on the grounds that this perpetuates and legitimates the existing system. Abolitionism proposes new responses to those who have been criminalised (including those irregularised by the state) and argues that the urge to punish and inflict pain must be challenged.

Chapter 5

1. In this chapter I focus on one actor in each city who worked to compose the meaning of sanctuary in a moment of friction, where governing systems seized up, and where meanings were destabilised. However, I do not want to diminish the roles of others, particularly those in immigrants' rights organisations. The economy of the book does not allow me to document the enormity of the work at the grassroots in all of these cities, which has been explored in detail by other scholars. It should also be borne in mind that I have chosen these moments as they emerged from my fieldwork. They are not representative or generalisable but rather point towards particular forms of the possible as windows into embedded practices.

2. City and County of San Francisco, Board of Supervisors Rules Committee 23 January 2019 Available at: https://sfgov.legistar.com/MeetingDetail.aspx?ID=672417&GUID=BF9E4483-9B26-420E-8A0B-4AAAA94CDCB0&Options=&Search= accessed 19 January 2022.

3. The issue had reached a crisis point because the federal government was shut down between 22 December 2018 and 25 January 2019 primarily because Democrats would not grant the Trump administration $5.7 billion to proceed with the construction of the wall on the US–Mexico border.

4. City and County of San Francisco Board of Supervisors Ordinance Number 190009 Available at City and County of San Francisco—File #: 190009 (legistar.com) accessed 19 January 2022.

5. Agenda item 35 'Authorizing Request for Parole Entry to the United States Department of Homeland Security'. Video between 3:04 and 3:17 hours. Available at: https://sanfrancisco.granicus.com/MediaPlayer.php?view_id=10&clip_id=32292 accessed 19 January 2022.

6. This is a public meeting and therefore names are not pseudonyms.

7. The local authorities were: Liverpool, Oxford, Brent, Croydon, Enfield, Islington, Hackney, Haringey, Lambeth, Newham, and Rugby (Mohdin 2019). This was in response to a report that the Greater London Authority shared data with the Home Office about non-UK rough sleepers to facilitate immigration control. Agreement obtained through FOIA by Liberty and reported on by *The Observer* (Townsend 2017).

8. A member of the national City of Sanctuary movement made an important point that many Cities of Sanctuary had applied for the 'Enforcement' strand of the

Controlling Migration Fund. She affirmed that the national City of Sanctuary framework is compatible with cooperation with national immigration enforcement.

9. Immigration and Refugee Board of Canada. Irregular border crosser statistics. Available at: https://irb-cisr.gc.ca/en/statistics/Pages/Irregular-border-crosser -statistics.aspx accessed 19 January 2022.

10. In Canada, the federal government's [partial] funding only begins once an individual enters the refugee determination process. In Ontario, the provincial government funds the income security system and the legal aid system for asylum seekers only under certain conditions.

11. Justin Trudeau. Twitter, 28 January 2017, 'To those fleeing persecution, terror & war, Canadians will welcome you, regardless of your faith. Diversity is our strength #WelcomeToCanada'. Available at: https://twitter.com/justintrudeau/status/ 825438460265762816?lang=en accessed 19 January 2022.

Conclusion

1. Scholars have framed questions around the rationales for 'sanctuary' broadly conceived and the implications that follow, but also foreground a description of 'sanctuary' and highlight sanctuary's radical potential and resistance. Here I focus specifically on the 'sanctuary city' and its political potentials and challenges and do not assume that sanctuary is implicitly about resistance or has disruptive effects.

2. An anti-immigrant organisation, Ohio Jobs and Justice PAC, began a website in 2007 that lists dozens of cities and localities that it considers sanctuary cities and those that have rescinded their designation. Steve Salvi, The Original List of Sanctuary Cities, USA. Available at: http://www.ojjpac.org/sanctuary.asp accessed 25 January 2022.

3. Immigration and Customs Enforcement 'Delegation of Immigration Authority Section 287(g) Immigration and Nationality Act'. Available at: https://www.ice.gov/ identify-and-arrest/287g accessed 12 April 2022.

4. AB-2792 Local law enforcement agencies: federal immigration policy enforcement: ICE access. Available at: https://leginfo.legislature.ca.gov/faces/billNavClient .xhtml?bill_id=201520160AB2792 accessed 12 April 2022.

5. AB-4 State government: federal immigration policy enforcement. Available at: https://leginfo.legislature.ca.gov/faces/billNavClient.xhtml?bill_id=201320140AB4 accessed 12 April 2022.

6. Sheffield City Council, Individual Cabinet Member Report. Refugee resettlement. 16 February 2016. Available at: https://democracy.sheffield.gov.uk/documents/ s21642/Refugee%20Resettlement.pdf accessed 23 September 2024.

Appendix 1

1. San Francisco Board of Supervisors Meeting Minutes and Journals of Proceedings from 1999 to 1906 Available at: https://sfbos.org/1999-1906 accessed 25 January 2022.

2. Including: the Public Defender's Office, the City Attorney, the Police and Fire departments, the Sheriff's Office, the department of Public Health, Juvenile and Adult Probation departments, the Human Services Agency (HSA), 311, Department of Emergency Communications, Department of Elections, Department of Parking and Traffic, the Rent Stabilization Board, and the Department of Public Transportation.

3. Including: Benefits; Parking; Schools and Childcare; Housing; Social Care; Disability and Mental Health; Parks, Sport and Recreation; Libraries and Archives; Pollution and Nuisance; Births, Deaths, Marriages and Citizenship; Public Health; Travel and Transport; South Yorkshire Police; Fire Department.

4. Including: 311 Toronto, Affordable Housing Office, Children's Services, City Manager's Office, Equity, Diversity, and Human Rights; Human Resources; and Strategic Communications, Court Services, Emergency Medical Services, Employment & Social Services, Facilities Management, Fire Services, Legal Services, Municipal Licensing and Standards, Parks, Forestry & Recreation, Public Health, Shelter, Support & Housing Administration, Social Development, Finance & Administration, Toronto Community Housing, Toronto Police Service, Toronto Public Library, Toronto Transit Commission.

5. I am hugely grateful to Angela Chan for facilitating my attendance at the Free SF meetings.

6. Including: Children's Peace Theatre, Fairview Community Health, FCJ Refugee Centre, Harriet Tubman Community Organization, Health for All, Hispanic Development ment Council, Immigration Legal Committee, Income Security Advocacy Centre, Law Office of Adela Crossley, Metro Toronto Chinese and Southeast Asian Legal Clinic, Migrant Workers Alliance for Change, Neighbourhood Link, Newcomer Women's Services Toronto, No One Is Illegal—Toronto, Ontario Council of Agencies Serving Immigrants (OCASI), Parkdale Community Legal Services, Social Planning Toronto, Solidarity City Network Toronto, South Asian Legal Clinic of Ontario, South Riverdale Community Health Centre, Thorncliffe Neighbourhood Office, Volunteer Health Clinic for the Uninsured, Warden Woods Local Immigration Partnership, Willowdale Community Legal Services, ACCES Employment, Agincourt Community Services Association, Canadian Centre for Victims of Torture, Catholic Crosscultural Services, For Youth Initiative, Laidlaw Foundation, Polycultural Immigrant & Community Services, St. Stephen's Community House, United Way Toronto & York Region, Warden Woods Community Centre, Wood Green Community Services, Working Women Community Centre, and YMCA of Greater Toronto.

7. The interviews cover the beginning of the sanctuary movement during the Vietnam conflict (1971–1972) and the more extensive movement assisting Central American refugees in the United States (1982–1987). This archive consisted of six boxes of materials.

8. Consisting of four boxes of materials.

9. Consisting of nine boxes and two folios of material.

10. Gus Schultz was a key figure in the sanctuary movement during this time. He was the pastor of the University Lutheran Chapel, Berkeley from 1969. He helped form the East Bay Sanctuary Covenant in March 1982 and helped to found, or was a member of, several other sanctuary-related organisations including the National Sanctuary Defense Fund, SHARE, and Salvadoran Humanitarian Aid among others. This collection includes three boxes of material and 1 folio of media reports.

Bibliography

Allen, John, and Allan Cochrane. "Beyond the Territorial Fix: Regional Assemblages, Politics and Power." *Regional Studies* 41, no. 9 (2007): 1161–75.

Allen, Tiffy *A Hundred Thousand Welcomes*. London: Lulu Publishers, 2020.

Anderson, Benedict. *Imagined Communities. Reflections on the Origin and Spread of Nationalism*. London: Verso Books, 1991.

Anderson, Bridget. *Us and Them?: The Dangerous Politics of Immigration Control*. Oxford University Press, 2013.

Anderson, Bridget, and Martin Ruhs. "Researching Illegality and Labour Migration." *Population, Space and Place* 16, no. 3 (2010): 175–79.

Appadurai, Arjun. "Introduction: Place and Voice in Anthropological Theory." *Cultural Anthropology* 3, no. 1 (1988): 16–20.

Armbruster, Heidi. "'It Was the Photograph of the Little Boy': Reflections on the Syrian Vulnerable Persons Resettlement Programme in the UK." *Ethnic and Racial Studies* 42, no. 15 (2019): 2680–99.

Armenta, Amada. *Protect, Serve, and Deport: The Rise of Policing as Immigration Enforcement*. University of California Press, 2017.

Askins, Kye. "Being Together: Everyday Geographies and the Quiet Politics of Belonging." *ACME: An International Journal for Critical Geographies* 14, no. 2 (2015): 470–478.

Atak, Idil. "The Criminalization of Migration in Canada and Its Unintended Policy Consequences." *The Oxford Handbook of Migration Crises* (2019): 467.

Avila, Lorena, and Sarah Tosh. "The Institutional Hearing Program and the Incarceration-to-Deportation Pipeline." *Critical Criminology* 32 (2024): 217–233. https://doi.org/10.1007/s10612-024-09783-3

Bagelman, Jennifer. *Sanctuary City: A Suspended State*. New York: Springer, 2016.

Baker, H. Robert. "The Fugitive Slave Clause and the Antebellum Constitution." *Law and History Review* 30, no. 4 (2012): 1133–1174.

Barder, Alexander. *Empire Within: International Hierarchy and its Imperial Laboratories of Governance*. Routledge, 2015.

Barth, Fredrik. "An Anthropology of Knowledge." *Current Anthropology* 43, no. 1 (2002): 1–18.

Baseler, Marilyn C. *"Asylum for Mankind": America, 1607–1800*. Cornell University Press, 1998.

Bau, Ignatius. *This Ground Is Holy: Church Sanctuary and Central American Refugees*. New Jersey: Paulist Press, 1985.

Bauman, Zygmunt. "Urban Space Wars: On Destructive Order and Creative Chaos." *Citizenship Studies* 3, no. 2 (1999): 173–85.

Benchekroun, Rachel, and Rachel Humphris. "U.K. Hostile Environment Resource Guide 1: What Is the Hostile Environment?" London: Social Scientists Against the Hostile Environment, 2021.

———. "U.K. Hostile Environment Resource Guide 2: Access to Health." London: Social Scientists Against the Hostile Environment, 2021.

Bhagat, Ali. "Governing Refugees in Raced Markets: Displacement and Disposability from Europe's Frontier to the Streets of Paris." *Review of International Political Economy* 29, no. 3 (2022): 955–978.

Bhattacharyya, Gargi. *Rethinking Racial Capitalism: Questions of Reproduction and Survival*. London: Rowman & Littlefield International, 2018.

Bradley, Gracie Mae. "Report: Care Don't Share." Liberty, 3 December 2018. Available at: https://www.libertyhumanrights.org.uk/issue/care-dont-share/ accessed 17 January 2022.

Brahinsky, Rachel. "Race and the Making of Southeast San Francisco: Towards a Theory of Race-Class." *Antipode* 46, no. 5 (2014): 1258–76.

Burr, Kathleen. "Local Immigration Partnerships: Building Welcoming and Inclusive Communities through Multi-Level Governance." *e-Horizons newsletter*. Policy Horizons Canada, 2011.

Busby, Mattha. "Immigration Check Outcry Sees Officers Removed by Councils." *Guardian*, 24 February 2019. Available at: https://www.theguardian.com/uk-news/2019/feb/24/labour-councils-remove-embedded-immigration-officers accessed 17 January 2022.

Button, Daniel, Akram Salhab, James Skinner, Aliya Yule and Kathryn Medien. "Patients Not Passports. Learning from the International Struggle for Universal Healthcare." New Economics Foundation, 15 October 2020. Available at: https://neweconomics.org/2020/10/patients-not-passports accessed 17 January 2022.

Button, Daniel, Akram Salhab, James Skinner, and Aliya Yule. *Patients Not Passports: Migrants' Access to Healthcare During the Coronavirus Crisis*. Medact, Migrants Organise, New Economics Foundation, June 2020. Available at: https://neweconomics.org/uploads/files/Patients-Not-Passports-Migrants-Access-to-Healthcare-During-the-Coronavirus-Crisis.pdf accessed 17 January 2022.

Calavita, Kitty. "'A Reserve Army of Delinquents' The Criminalization and Economic Punishment of Immigrants in Spain." *Punishment & Society* 5, no. 4 (2003): 399–413.

Castles, Stephen, and Alastair Davidson. *Citizenship and Migration: Globalization and the Politics of Belonging*. Psychology Press, 2000.

Chakrabarty, Dipesh. *Provincializing Europe*. New Jersey: Princeton University Press, 2000.

Chauvin, Sébastien, and Blanca Garcés-Mascareñas. "Beyond Informal Citizenship: The New Moral Economy of Migrant Illegality." *International Political Sociology* 6, no. 3 (2012): 241–59.

City of Sanctuary. "2014 Sanctuary Summit Communiqué: The Birmingham Declaration", 15 November 2014. Available at: https://www.cityofsanctuary.org/files/the _birmingham_declaration_-nov-15th1_0.pdf accessed 21 January 2022.

City of Toronto. "2021 Census Backgrounder" (4 November 2022). Available at: https:// www.toronto.ca/wp-content/uploads/2023/03/8ff2-2021-Census-Backgrounder -Immigration-Ethnoracial-Mobility-Migration-Religion-FINAL1.1-corrected.pdf accessed 14 November 2023.

Clarke, John, Dave Bainton, Noemi Lendvai, and Paul Stubbs. *Making Policy Move: Towards a Politics of Translation and Assemblage*. Bristol: Policy Press, 2015.

Clarke, John, and Janet Newman. *The Managerial State: Power, Politics and Ideology in the Remaking of Social Welfare*. Sage, 1997.

Clavel, Pierre, and Robert Kraushaar. "On Being Unreasonable: Progressive Planning in Sheffield and Chicago." *International Planning Studies* 3, no. 2 (1998): 143–62.

Cohen, Cathy J. *The Boundaries of Blackness: Aids and the Breakdown of Black Politics*. University of Chicago Press, 1999.

Comaroff, John L. "Reflections on the Colonial State, in South Africa and Elsewhere: Factions, Fragments, Facts and Fictions." *Social Identities* 4, no. 3 (1998): 321–61.

Coutin, Susan Bibler. *The Culture of Protest: Religious Activism and the US Sanctuary Movement*. Boulder, Colorado: Westview Press, 1993.

Cross, Hannah. *Migration Beyond Capitalism*. John Wiley & Sons, 2020.

Cross, Malcolm, and Michael Keith, eds. *Racism, the City and the State*. London: Routledge, 1993.

Cunningham, Hilary. *God and Caesar at the Rio Grande: Sanctuary and the Politics of Religion*. Minneapolis: University of Minnesota Press, 1995.

Cvajner, Martina, and Giuseppe Sciortino. "Theorizing Irregular Migration: The Control of Spatial Mobility in Differentiated Societies." *European Journal of Social Theory* 13, no. 3 (2010): 389–404.

Da Costa, Melanie Eduarda. *Toronto Police Services: Ethics and Practices That May Lead to Deportation*. Toronto: University of Toronto, 2020.

Damer, Seán. "'Engineers of the Human Machine': The Social Practice of Council Housing Management in Glasgow, 1895–1939." *Urban Studies* 37, no. 11 (2000): 2007–26.

Danewid, Ida. "The Fire This Time: Grenfell, Racial Capitalism and the Urbanisation of Empire." *European Journal of International Relations* 26, no. 1 (2020): 289–313.

———. "White Innocence in the Black Mediterranean: Hospitality and the Erasure of History." *Third World Quarterly* 38, no. 7 (2017): 1674–89.

Darling, Jonathan. "A City of Sanctuary: The Relational Re-Imagining of Sheffield's Asylum Politics." *Transactions of the Institute of British Geographers* 35, no. 1 (2010): 125–40.

Davis, David Brion. *Inhuman Bondage: The Rise and Fall of Slavery in the New World*. Oxford: Oxford University Press, 2006.

DeBenedetti, Katie. "San Francisco Declares Itself a Transgender Sanctuary City." *KQED*, 12 June 2024. Available at: https://www.kqed.org/news/11989910/ san-francisco-declares-itself-a-transgender-sanctuary-city accessed 14 June 2024.

De Graauw, Els. *Making Immigrant Rights Real: Nonprofits and the Politics of Integration in San Francisco*. Cornell University Press, 2016.

Desmond, Matthew. "Eviction and the Reproduction of Urban Poverty." *American Journal of Sociology* 118, no. 1 (2012): 88–133.

Diamond, Patrick. *The British Labour Party in Opposition and Power 1979–2019: Forward March Halted?* Routledge, 2021.

Dobrowolsky, Alexandra, and Ruth Lister. "Eight: Social Investment: The Discourse and the Dimensions of Change." In *Modernising the Welfare State*, edited by Michael Powell. Bristol, UK: Policy Press, 2008. https://doi.org/10.51952/ 9781847423665.ch008

Dürr, Eveline, Moritz Ege, Johannes Moser, Christoph K. Neumann, and Gordon M. Winder. "Urban Ethics: Towards a Research Agenda on Cities, Ethics and Normativity." *City, Culture and Society* 20 (2020): 100313.

Düvell, Franck. "Paths into Irregularity: The Legal and Political Construction of Irregular Migration." *European Journal of Migration and Law* 13, no. 3 (2011): 275–295.

Els de, Graauw. "Municipal Id Cards for Undocumented Immigrants: Local Bureaucratic Membership in a Federal System." *Politics & Society* 42, no. 3 (2014): 309–30.

Fassin, Didier. *Humanitarian Reason: A Moral History of the Present*. University of California Press, 2011.

Fox, Cybelle. *Three Worlds of Relief: Race, Immigration, and Public and Private Social Welfare Spending in American Cities*. New Jersey: Princeton University Press, 2012.

———. "Unauthorized Welfare: The Origins of Immigrant Status Restrictions in American Social Policy." *Journal of American History* 102, no. 4 (2016): 1051–74.

———. "City Council to Reaffirm Toronto's Status as a Sanctuary City," CTV, 31 January 2017. Available at: https://toronto.ctvnews.ca/city-council-to-reaffirm-toronto -s-status-as-a-sanctuary-city-1.3265223 accessed 21 January 2022.

Frisken, Frances. *The Public Metropolis: The Political Dynamics of Urban Expansion in the Toronto Region, 1924–2003*. Ottawa: Canadian Scholars' Press, 2007.

Frost, Nick. *Rethinking Children and Families: The Relationship between Childhood, Families and the State*. A&C Black, 2011.

Frug Gerald, E. "The city as a legal concept." *Harvard Law Review* 93.6 (1980): 1057–154.

Furman, Rich, Alissa R. Ackerman, Melody Loya, Susanna Jones, and Nalinin Egi. "The Criminalization of Immigration: Value Conflicts for the Social Work Profession." *Journal of Sociology and Social Welfare* 39, no. 1 (2012): 169.

Gastaldo, Denise, Christine Carrasco, and Lilian Magalhaes. "Undocumented Workers in Ontario." Migration as a Social Determinant of Health, 2012. Available at https://www.migrationhealth.ca/undocumented-workers-ontario accessed 14 November 2023.

Geertz, Clifford. *The Interpretation of Cultures.* Vol. 5019: Basic books, 1973.

Gentleman, Amelia. "Right to Rent Rule 'Justified' Finds UK Appeal Court." *Guardian*, 21 April 2020. Available at: https://www.theguardian.com/politics/2020/apr/21/right-to-rent-rule-justified-finds-uk-appeal-court accessed 17 January 2022.

Gilmore, Ruth Wilson. *Golden Gulag: Prisons, Surplus, Crisis, and Opposition in Globalizing California.* Vol. 21: University of California Press, 2007.

Goldberg, David Theo. *The Racial State.* Blackwell Publishing, 2002.

Grayson, John. "Explaining and Learning from the UKIP surge in South Yorkshire." Institute of Race Relations, 5 June 2014. Available at: https://irr.org.uk/article/explaining-and-learning-from-the-ukip-surge-in-south-yorkshire/ accessed 14 November 2023.

Guttentag, Lucas. "The Forgotten Equality Norm in Immigration Preemption: Discrimination, Harassment, and the Civil Rights Act of 1870." *Duke Journal of Constitutional Law and Public Policy* 8, no. 2 (2013): 40–51.

Habal, Estella. *San Francisco's International Hotel: Mobilizing the Filipino American Community in the Anti-Eviction Movement.* Temple University Press, 2007.

Hall, Stuart. "Gramsci and Us." In *The Hard Road to Renewal: Thatcherism and the Crisis of the Left*, edited by Stuart Hall. London: Verso, 1988.

Hanieh, Adam. "The Contradictions of Global Migration." *Socialist Register* 55 (2019): 50–78.

Hart, Angela. "Gavin Newsom Admits He Was Wrong to Report Young Immigrants to ICE as Mayor." *The Mercury News*, 20 July 2018. Available at: https://www.mercurynews.com/2018/07/20/gavin-newsom-admits-he-was-wrong-to-report-young-immigrants-to-ice-as-mayor/ accessed 14 February 2022.

Hart, Gillian. "Relational Comparison Revisited: Marxist Postcolonial Geographies in Practice." *Progress in Human Geography* 42, no. 3 (2018): 371–94.

Hartman, Chester, and Sarah Carnochan. *City for Sale: The Transformation of San Francisco.* University of California Press, 2002.

Hershkowitz, Mia, Graham Hudson, and Harald Bauder. "Rescaling the Sanctuary City: Police and Non-Status Migrants in Ontario, Canada." *International Migration* 59, no. 1 (2021): 38–57.

Hill, Amelia and Diane Taylor. "Right to Rent Scheme Ruled Incompatible with Human Rights Law." *The Guardian*, 1 March 2019. Available at: https://www.theguardian.com/uk-news/2019/mar/01/right-to-rent-scheme-ruled-incompatible-with-human-rights-law accessed 17 January 2022.

Hill Collins, Patricia. "The New Politics of Community." *American Sociological Review* 75, no. 1 (2010): 7–30.

Hirota, Hidetaka. *Expelling the Poor: Atlantic Seaboard States and the Nineteenth-Century Origins of American Immigration Policy.* Oxford: Oxford University Press, 2016.

Holmes, Seth M., and Heide Castañeda. "Representing the 'European Refugee Crisis' in Germany and Beyond: Deservingness and Difference, Life and Death." *American Ethnologist* 43, no. 1 (2016): 12–24.

Home, Robert. *Of Planting and Planning: The Making of British Colonial Cities.* London: Spon, 1997.

Homeless Link (2024) *Briefing: Facing up to homelessness among non-UK nationals.* 2 February 2024. Available at https://homeless.org.uk/knowledge-hub/local-solutions-to-non-uk-national-homelessness/ accessed 18 September 2024.

Hughes, Vanessa. "Child Migrants' Right to Education in a London Academy: Tensions Between Policy, Language Provision, and International Standards." *Human Rights Education Review* 4, no. 1 (2021): 70–90.

Humphris, Rachel. *A History of the Memories of the Sanctuary City in Toronto, Canada.* Toronto: Ryerson Centre for Immigration and Settlement (RCIS), 2020a.

———. *Sheffield: A History of Memories of the "Sanctuary City".* IRiS Working Paper Series. University of Birmingham, 2020b.

———. *Home-Land: Romanian Roma, Domestic Spaces and the State.* Bristol: Bristol University Press, 2019a.

———. "Mutating Faces of the State? Austerity, Migration and Faith-Based Volunteers in a UK Downscaled Urban Context." *The Sociological Review* 67, no. 1 (2019b): 95–110.

———. *San Francisco: A History of Memories of the "Sanctuary City".* Welcoming Cities Working Paper, Queen Mary University of London, 2021.

Humphris, Rachel, and Kristin Elizabeth Yarris. "Welcoming Acts: Temporality and Affect Among Volunteer Humanitarians in the UK and USA." *Migration and Society* 5, no. 1 (2022): 75–89.

Independent Chief Inspector of Borders and Immigration. *An Inspection of the 'Hostile Environment' Measures Relating to Driving Licences and Bank Accounts January to July 2016.* October 2016. Available at: https://www.gov.uk/government/uploads/system/uploads/attachment_data/file/567652/ICIBI-hostile-environment-driving-licences-and-bank-accounts-January-to-July-2016.pdf accessed 17 January 2022.

———. *An Inspection of Home Office (Borders, Immigration and Citizenship System) Collaborative Working with Other Government Departments and Agencies. February–October 2018.* January 2019. Available at: https://assets.publishing.service.gov.uk/government/uploads/system/uploads/attachment_data/file/774736/An_inspection_of_Home_Office_collaborative_working_with_OGDs_and_agencies_web_version.pdf accessed 17 January 2022.

Isin, Engin Fahri. *Being Political: Genealogies of Citizenship.* Minneapolis: University of Minnesota Press, 2002.

———. "Introduction: Cities and Citizenship in a Global Age." *Citizenship Studies* 3, no. 2 (1999): 165–71.

———. *Cities without Citizens: Modernity of the City as a Corporation.* Black Rose Books, 1992.

———. *The Birth of the Modern City in British North America: An Introduction,* Research Paper, no. 173. University of Toronto, Centre for Urban and Community Studies, 1989.

Isin, Engin Fahri, and Evelyn Sharon Ruppert. *Being Digital Citizens.* Rowman & Littlefield Publishers, 2015.

Isin, Engin Fahri, and Patricia K. Wood. *Citizenship and Identity.* London: Sage Publications, 1999.

James, Ryan K. "From 'Slum Clearance' to 'Revitalisation': Planning, Expertise and Moral Regulation in Toronto's Regent Park." *Planning Perspectives* 25 no. 1 (2010): 69–86.

Joint Council for the Welfare of Immigrants. "Who are the UK's Undocumented Population?" (June 2024). Available at: https://www.jcwi.org.uk/who-are-the-uks-undocumented-population accessed 14 November 2023.

Jones, Chris. *Data Protection, Immigration Enforcement and Fundamental Rights: What the EU's Regulations on Interoperability Mean for People with Irregular Status.* PICUM, 2019. Available at: https://picum.org/wp-content/uploads/2019/11/Data-Protection-Immigration-Enforcement-and-Fundamental-Rights-Full-Report-EN.pdf accessed 17 January 2022.

Kanazawa, Mark. "Immigration, Exclusion, and Taxation: Anti-Chinese Legislation in Gold Rush California." *The Journal of Economic History* 65, no. 3 (2005): 779–805.

Kanstroom, Dan. *Deportation Nation: Outsiders in American History.* Harvard University Press, 2007.

Kapoor, Nisha. *Deport, Deprive, Extradite: 21st Century State Extremism.* Verso Books, 2018.

Katz, Michael B. *Improving Poor People: The Welfare State, the "Underclass," and Urban Schools as History.* Princeton University Press, 1997.

Kelley, Ninette, and Michael J. Trebilcock. *The Making of the Mosaic: A History of Canadian Immigration Policy.* University of Toronto Press, 2000.

Kubal, Agnieszka. "Conceptualizing Semi-legality in Migration Research." *Law & Society Review* 47, no. 3 (2013): 555–587.

Kurnik, Andrej, and Maple Razsa. "Reappropriating the Balkan Route: Mobility Struggles and Joint-Agency in Bosnia and Herzegovina." *Two Homelands* 52 (2020). Available at: http://twohomelands.zrc-sazu.si/en/articles/show/623/reappropriating-the-balkan-route-mobility-struggles-and-joint-agency-in-bosnia-and-herzegovina

Lange, Matthew, et al. "Colonialism and Development: A Comparative Analysis of Spanish and British Colonies." *American Journal of Sociology*, vol. 111, no. 5, 2006, pp. 1412–62. *JSTOR*, https://doi.org/10.1086/499510.

Landolt, Patricia. "Assembling the Local Politics of Noncitizenship: Contesting Access to Healthcare in Toronto-Sanctuary City." *Social Problems* 69, no. 1 (2022): 74–90.

Landolt, Patricia, and Luin Goldring. "Assembling Noncitizen Access to Education in a Sanctuary City: The Place of Public School Administrator Bordering Practices." In *Accountability across Borders: Migrant Rights in North America*, edited by Bada Xóchitl and Gleeson Shannon. Austin: University of Texas Press, 2021.

Lasch, Christopher N., R. Linus Chan, Ingrid V. Eagly, Dina Francesca Haynes, Annie Lai, Elizabeth M. McCormick, and Juliet P. Stumpf. "Understanding Sanctuary Cities." *Boston College Law Review* 59, no. 5 (2018): 1703–74.

Latour, Bruno. *Pandora's Hope: Essays on the Reality of Science Studies.* Harvard University Press, 1999.

Law, Anna O. "Lunatics, Idiots, Paupers, and Negro Seamen—Immigration Federalism and the Early American State." *Studies in American Political Development* 28, no. 2 (2014): 107–28.

Lee, Stacy J. *Unraveling the "Model Minority" Stereotype: Listening to Asian American Youth.* Teachers College Press, 2015.

Legg, Stephen, and Colin McFarlane. "Ordinary Urban Spaces: Between Postcolonialism and Development." *Environment and Planning A* 40 no. 1 (2008): 6–14.

Leo, Christopher, and Martine August. "The Multilevel Governance of Immigration and Settlement: Making Deep Federalism Work." *Canadian Journal of Political Science/Revue canadienne de science politique* 42, no. 2 (2009): 491–510.

Levitz, Philip, and Grigore Pop-Eleches. "Monitoring, Money and Migrants: Countering Post-Accession Backsliding in Bulgaria and Romania." *Europe-Asia Studies* 62, no. 3 (2010): 461–79.

Liberty. "Data Watchdog Slams Department for Education for Mishandling Children's Data after Liberty Legal Action." 13 November 2019. Available at: https://www.libertyhumanrights.org.uk/issue/data-watchdog-slams-dfe-for-mishandling-childrens-data-after-liberty-legal-action/ accessed 17 January 2022.

Long, Percy V. "Consolidated City and County Government of San Francisco." *Proceedings of the American Political Science Association* 8 (1911): 109–21. https://doi.org/10.2307/3038399

Low, Setha M. "The Anthropology of Cities: Imagining and Theorizing the City." Annual Review of Anthropology 25 no. 1 (1996): 383–409.

Madanipour, Ali, Konrad Miciukiewicz, and Geoff Vigar. "Master Plans and Urban Change: The Case of Sheffield City Centre." *Journal of Urban Design* 23, no. 4 (2018): 465–81.

Magnusson, Warren. *The Search for Political Space.* Toronto: University of Toronto Press 1996.

Maharawal, Manissa M. "Black Lives Matter, Gentrification and the Security State in the San Francisco Bay Area." *Anthropological Theory* 17, no. 3 (2017): 338–64.

Malkki, Liisa H. *The Need to Help: The Domestic Arts of International Humanitarianism.* Duke University Press, 2015.

Mancina, Peter. "In the Spirit of Sanctuary: Sanctuary-City Policy Advocacy and the Production of Sanctuary-Power in San Francisco, California." PhD diss., Vanderbilt University, 2016.

———. "Investigating and (Not) Disciplining Violations of Sanctuary City Laws." *Southern California Interdisciplinary Law Journal* 28 (2018): 641.

Marcus, George E. "Ethnography in/of the World System: The Emergence of Multi-Sited Ethnography." *Annual Review of Anthropology* 24 (1995): 95–117.

Marcuse, Peter. "Gentrification, Social Justice and Personal Ethics." *International Journal of Urban and Regional Research* 39, no. 6 (2015): 1263–69.

Marrow, Helen B. "Deserving to a Point: Unauthorized Immigrants in San Francisco's Universal Access Healthcare Model." *Social Science & Medicine* 74, no. 6 (2012): 846–854.

Martin, Shelby Joy. "Creating a Culture of Care: Navigating the Politics of Life and Death in the Clinical Setting." University of Toronto, 5 April 2020. Available at: https://rnswn.files.wordpress.com/2020/06/martin-2020-creating-a-culture-of-care.pdf accessed 17 January 2022.

Massey, Doreen. "Power-Geometry and a Progressive Sense of Place." In *Mapping the Futures: Local Cultures, Global Change*, edited by Jon Bird, Barry Curtis, Tim Putnam, George Robertson and Lisa Tuckner, 59–69. London/New York: Routledge, 1993.

Maynard, Robyn. *Policing Black Lives: State Violence in Canada from Slavery to the Present.* Fernwood Publishing, 2017.

McCann, Eugene, and Kevin Ward. "Assembling Urbanism: Following Policies and 'Studying through' the Sites and Situations of Policy Making." *Environment and Planning A: Economy and Space* 44, no. 1 (2012): 42–51.

McClintock, Anne. "Imperial Leather: Race, Gender, and Sexuality in the Colonial Contest." New York: Routledge, 1995.

McElroy, Erin. "Data, Dispossession, and Facebook: Techno-Imperialism and Toponymy in Gentrifying San Francisco." *Urban Geography* 40, no. 6 (2019): 826–45.

McElroy, Erin, and Alex Werth. "Deracinated Dispossessions: On the Foreclosures of 'Gentrification' in Oakland, Ca." *Antipode* 51, no. 3 (2019): 878–98.

Mezzadra, Sandro, and Brett Neilson. "Between Inclusion and Exclusion: On the Topology of Global Space and Borders." *Theory, Culture & Society* 29, no. 4–5 (2012): 58–75.

Midgley, James. "Imperialism, Colonialism and Social Welfare." In *Colonialism and Welfare: Social Policy and British Imperial Legacy*, edited by James Midgley and David Piachaud, 36–54. London: Edward Elgar Publishing, 2011.

————. "Poor Law Principles and Social Assistance in the Third World: A Study of the Perpetuation of Colonial Welfare." *International Social Work* 27, no. 1 (1984): 19–29.

Mignolo, Walter *The Darker Side of the Renaissance: Literacy, Territoriality, and Colonization*. University of Michigan Press, 2003.

Mirabal, Nancy Raquel. "Geographies of Displacement: Latina/os, Oral History, and the Politics of Gentrification in San Francisco's Mission District." *The Public Historian* 31, no. 2 (2009): 7–31.

Mitchell, Timothy. "The Limits of the State: Beyond Statist Approaches and Their Critics." *American Political Science Review* 85, no. 1 (1991): 77–96.

Mohdin, Aamna. "Councils Refusing to Reveal Data of Rough Sleepers to Home Office." *Guardian*, 17 July 2019. Available at: https://www.theguardian.com/society/2019/jul/17/councils-refusing-to-share-personal-data-of-rough-sleepers-with-home-office accessed 17 January 2022.

Molnar, Petra. *Technological Testing Grounds: Migration Management Experiments and Reflections from the Ground Up*. EDRI, November 2020. Available at: https://edri.org/wp-content/uploads/2020/11/Technological-Testing-Grounds.pdf accessed 17 January 2022.

Mosse, David. *Cultivating Development: An Ethnography of Aid Policy and Practice*. London: Abe Books, 2004.

Mosse, David, and David Lewis. "Theoretical Approaches to Brokerage and Translation in Development." In *Development Brokers and Translators: The Ethnography of Aid and Agencies*, edited by David Mosse and David Lewis. London: Kumarian Press, 2006.

Motomura, Hiroshi. "The Rights of Others: Legal Claims and Immigration Outside the Law." *Duke Law Journal* 59 (2010): 1723–1786.

————. *Immigration Outside the Law*. Oxford: Oxford University Press, 2014.

Muehlebach, Andrea Karin. *The Moral Neoliberal: Welfare and Citizenship in Italy*. University of Chicago Press, 2012.

Murray Li, Tania. "Practices of Assemblage and Community Forest Management." *Economy and Society* 36, no. 2 (2007): 263–93.

Narita, Kaelynn. "An Infrastructural Approach to the Digital Hostile Environment." *Journal of Global Ethics* 19, no. 3 (2023): 294–306. https://doi.org/10.1080/17449626.2023.2272773

National Immigration Law Center. "How California Driver's License Records Are Shared with the Department of Homeland Security." December 2018. Available at: https://www.nilc.org/issues/immigration-enforcement/how-calif-dl-records-shared-with-dhs/ accessed 17 January 2022.

Neuman, Gerald L. *Strangers to the Constitution: Immigrants, Borders, and Fundamental Law*. Princeton University Press, 1996.

Nightingale, Carl H. *Segregation: A Global History of Divided Cities*. University of Chicago Press, 2012.

No Recourse to Public Funds Network. "Accessing and supporting adults who have no recourse to public funds (England) Housing and Welfare Rights." 16 March 2023. Available at https://guidance.nrpfnetwork.org.uk/reader/practice-guidance-adults/ accessed 18 September 2024.

Opillard, Florian. "Resisting the Politics of Displacement in the San Francisco Bay Area: Anti-Gentrification Activism in the Tech Boom 2.0." *European Journal of American Studies* 10, no. 10–3 (2015).

Pallister-Wilkins, Polly. "Hotspots and the Geographies of Humanitarianism." *Environment and Planning D: Society and Space* 38, no. 6 (2020): 991–1008.

Palmer, Colin A. *The Worlds of Unfree Labour: From Indentured Servitude to Slavery.* Rugby: Variorum, 1998.

Peake, Linda, and Martina Rieker. *Rethinking Feminist Interventions into the Urban.* Routledge, 2013.

Peck, Jamie. "Geographies of Policy: From Transfer-Diffusion to Mobility-Mutation." *Progress in Human Geography* 35, no. 6 (2011): 773–97.

Picker, Giovanni, Karim Murji, and Manuela Boatcă. "Racial Urbanities: Towards a Global Cartography." Social Identities 25, no. 1 (2019): 1–10.

Prak, Maarten. *Citizens without Nations: Urban Citizenship in Europe and the World, c.1000–1789.* Cambridge: Cambridge University Press, 2018.

Price, David. *Sheffield Troublemakers: Rebels and Radicals in Sheffield History.* London: Phillimore, 2011.

Pulido, Laura. "Rethinking Environmental Racism: White Privilege and Urban Development in Southern California." *Annals of the Association of American Geographers* 90, no. 1 (2000): 12–40.

Rabinow, Paul. "Governing Morocco: Modernity and Difference." *International Journal of Urban and Regional Research* 13, no. 1 (1989): 32–46.

Ravetz, Alison. *Council Housing and Culture: The History of a Social Experiment.* London: Routledge, 2003.

Ritchie, Andrea J. "Race, Migration and Policing." Presented at Sanctuary: What's Next? An International Forum for, with and by Undocumented Migrants, Ryerson University, 5 November 2020.

Robinson, Cedric J. *Black Marxism: The Making of the Black Radical Tradition.* Chapel Hill: University of North Carolina Press, 1983.

Rose, Nikolas. *Powers of Freedom: Reframing Political Thought.* Cambridge University Press, 1999.

Rothstein, Richard. *The Color of Law: A Forgotten History of How Our Government Segregated America.* Liveright Publishing, 2017.

Rousseau, Max. "Re-Imaging the City Centre for the Middle Classes: Regeneration, Gentrification and Symbolic Policies in 'Loser Cities'." *International Journal of Urban and Regional Research* 33, no. 3 (2009): 770–88

Roy, Ananya. "The City in the Age of Trumpism: From Sanctuary to Abolition." *Environment and Planning D: Society and Space* 37, no. 5 (2019): 761–778.

San Francisco Anti-Displacement Coalition. *San Francisco's Eviction Crisis 2015: A Report by SFADC.* San Francisco: San Francisco Anti-Displacement Coalition, 2015. http://antievictionmappingproject.net/evictionsurge.html

Sassen, Saskia. *Expulsions.* Harvard University Press, 2014.

Saunt, Claudio. *Unworthy Republic: The Dispossession of Native Americans and the Road to Indian Territory.* New York: WW Norton & Company, 2020.

Schweik, Susan M. *The Ugly Laws: Disability in Public.* New York: New York University Press, 2009.

Scott, James C. *Seeing Like a State: How Certain Schemes to Improve the Human Condition Have Failed.* Yale Agrarian Studies. New Haven: Yale University Press, 1998.

Seekings, Jeremy. "The Beveridge Report, the Colonial Office, and Welfare Reform in British Colonies." Unpublished paper. University of Cape Town, 2013.

San Francisco Rent Board. *Rent Board Annual Statistical Report.* San Francisco: San Francisco Rent Board, 2016. http://sfrb.org/rent-board-annual-statistical-report

Sheffield City Council. *Sheffield City Council Revenue Budget 2023/24* (March 2023). Available at: https://democracy.sheffield.gov.uk/documents/s57829/3.%20Revenue%20Budget%20Report%202023-24.pdf accessed 14 November 2012.

Sheringham, Olivia, and Helen Taylor. "On Stories, Storytelling, and the Quiet Politics of Welcome." *ACME: An International E-Journal for Critical Geographies* 21, no. 3 (2022): 284–302.

Shilliam, Robbie. *Race and the Undeserving Poor: From Abolition to Brexit.* Agenda Publishing, 2018.

Shore, Cris, and Susan Wright. *Policy: A New Field of Anthropology.* London: Routledge, 1997.

Shore, Cris, Susan Wright, and Davide Però. *Policy Worlds: Anthropology and the Analysis of Contemporary Power.* Vol. 14. Berghahn Books, 2011.

Siddons, Edward, and Niamh McIntyre. "Home Office Staff Sit in on Council Interviews with Migrant Families." *Guardian,* 28 October 2018. Available at: https://www.theguardian.com/uk-news/2018/oct/28/home-office-staff-sit-in-on-council-interviews-with-migrant-families accessed 17 January 2022.

Sinclair, Georgina, and Chris A. Williams. "'Home and Away': The Cross-fertilisation Between 'Colonial' and 'British' Policing, 1921–85." *Journal of Imperial and Commonwealth History* 35, no. 2 (2007): 221–238.

Slaven, Mike. "The Windrush Scandal and the Individualization of Postcolonial Immigration Control in Britain." *Ethnic and Racial Studies* 45, no. 16 (2021): 49–71. https://doi.org/10.1080/01419870.2021.2001555

Smith, Stacey L. *Freedom's Frontier: California and the Struggle over Unfree Labor, Emancipation, and Reconstruction.* Chapel Hill: University of North Carolina Books, 2013.

Solnit, Rebecca, and Susan Schwartzenberg. *Hollow City: The Siege of San Francisco and the Crisis of American Urbanism.* Verso, 2000.

Sparks, Richard, Evi Girling, and Ian Loader. "Fear and Everyday Urban Lives." *Urban Studies* 38, no. 5–6 (2001): 885–98.

Spivak, Gayatri Chakravorty. "Neocolonialism and the Secret Agent of Knowledge." *Oxford Literary Review* 13, no. 1 (1991): 220–51.

Squire, Vicki, and Jonathan Darling. "The 'Minor' Politics of Rightful Presence: Justice and Relationality in City of Sanctuary." *International Political Sociology* 7, no. 1 (2013): 59–74.

Staeheli, Lynn A., and Albert Thompson. "Citizenship, Community, and Struggles for Public Space." *The Professional Geographer* 49 no. 1 (1997): 28–38. https://doi.org/10.1111/0033-0124.00053

Stoler, Ann Laura. "Rethinking Colonial Categories: European Communities and the Boundaries of Rule." *Comparative Studies in Society and History* 31, no. 1 (1989): 134–61.

Stoler, Ann Laura, and Frederick Cooper. "Between Metropole and Colony." In *Tensions of Empire: Colonial Cultures in a Bourgeois World*, edited by Ann Laura Stoler and Frederick Cooper, 1–56. University of California Press, 1997.

Storper, Michael, and Allen J Scott. "Current Debates in Urban Theory: A Critical Assessment." *Urban Studies* 53, no. 6 (2016): 1114–36.

Strazzari, Davide. "Immigration and Federalism in Canada: Beyond Quebec Exceptionalism?". *Perspectives on Federalism* 9, no. 3 (2017): 56–84.

SYMAAG. "Sheffield: Hostile Environment or City of Sanctuary?" 8 August 2019. Available at: https://www.symaag.org.uk/sheffield-hostile-environment-or-city-of-sanctuary/2091/ accessed 19 January 2022.

Teaford, Jon C. *The Municipal Revolution in America: Origins of Modern Urban Government, 1650–1825.* Chicago, The University of Chicago Press, 1975.

Ticktin, Miriam I. *Casualties of Care: Immigration and the Politics of Humanitarianism in France.* Oakland: University of California Press, 2011.

Tolley, Erin, and Robert Young. *Immigrant Settlement Policy in Canadian Municipalities.* Montreal: McGill-Queen's Press, 2011.

Townsend, Mark. "Home Office Used Charity Data Map to Deport Rough Sleepers." *Observer*, 19 August 2017. Available at: https://www.theguardian.com/uk-news/2017/aug/19/home-office-secret-emails-data-homeless-eu-nationals accessed 17 January 2022.

Trattner, Walter I. *From Poor Law to Welfare State: A History of Social Welfare in America.* Simon and Schuster, 1989.

UK Home Office. "Landlord's guide to right to rent checks." 21 June 2024. Available at: https://assets.publishing.service.gov.uk/media/66744434c087fbe40855cece/Landlords_Guidance_March_2024_onwards__1_.pdf accessed 18 September 2024.

Valverde, Mariana. "Games of Jurisdiction: How Local Governance Realities Challenge the 'Creatures of the Province' Doctrine." *Journal of Law and Social Policy* 34 (2021): 21–38.

Villegas, Francisco J. "'Don't Ask, Don't Tell': Examining the Illegalization of Undocumented Students in Toronto, Canada." *British Journal of Sociology of Education* 39, no. 8 (2018): 1111–25.

———. "'Access without Fear!': Reconceptualizing 'Access' to Schooling for Undocumented Students in Toronto." *Critical Sociology* 43, no. 7–8 (2016): 1179–95.

———. "Getting to 'Don't Ask Don't Tell' at the Toronto District School Board: Mapping the Competing Discourses of Rights and Membership." In *Producing and Negotiating Non-Citizenship: Precarious Legal Status in Canada*, edited by Luin Goldring and Patricia Landolt. Toronto: University of Toronto Press, 2013.

Walker, Richard, and Alex Schafran. "The Strange Case of the Bay Area." *Environment and Planning A* 47, no. 1 (2015): 10–29.

Wangari-Jones, Peninah, Laura Loyola-Hernández, and Rachel Humphris. *STOP THE SCAN: Police Use of Mobile Fingerprinting Technology for Immigration Enforcement, UK*. Racial Justice Network and Yorkshire Resists, 2021. Available at: https://racialjusticenetwork.co.uk/wp-content/uploads/2021/06/stop-the-scan-report.pdf accessed 18 September 2024.

Watters, Charles. "Refugees at Europe's Borders: The Moral Economy of Care." *Transcultural Psychiatry* 44, no. 3 (2007): 394–417.

Weber, Max 1922. "The city (non-legitimate domination)." In *Economy and Society: An Outline of Interpretive Sociology*, translated by E. Fischoff, H. Gerth, A.M. Henderson, F. Kolegar, C.W. Mills, T. Parsons, M. Rheinstein, G. Roth, E. Shils and C. Wittich., edited by Guenther Roth and Claus Wittich. Berkeley: University of California Press (1958) 2 vols. Vol.2, ch. XVI: 1212–372.

Wemyss, Georgie. "'Compliant Environment': Turning Ordinary People into Border Guards Should Concern Everyone in the UK." *The Conversation*, 20 November 2018. Available at: https://theconversation.com/compliant-environment-turning-ordinary-people-into-border-guards-should-concern-everyone-in-the-uk-107066 accessed 17 January 2022.

Winant, Howard. *The New Politics of Race: Globalism, Difference, Justice*. Minnesota: University of Minnesota Press, 2004.

Winks, Robin W. "Slavery, the Loyalists, and English Canada, 1760–1801." In *The History of Immigration and Racism in Canada: Essential Readings*, edited by Barrington Walker. Ottawa Canadian Scholars Press, 2008.

Wolf, Eric R. "Anthropology among the Powers." *Social Anthropology* 7, no. 2 (1999): 121–34.

Worpole, Ken. *Here Comes the Sun: Architecture and Public Space in Twentieth-Century European Culture*. Reaktion books, 2000.

Wright, Gwendolyn. *The Politics of Design in French Colonial Urbanism*. Chicago: University of Chicago Press, 1991.

Wright, Susan, and Sue Reinhold. "'Studying Through': A Strategy for Studying Political Transformation. Or Sex, Lies and British Politics." In *Policy Worlds: Anthropology and the Analysis of Contemporary Power*, edited by Cris Shore, Susan Wright and Davide Però. London: Berghahn Books, 2011.

Young, Iris Marion. "Polity and Group Difference: A Critique of the Ideal of Universal Citizenship." *Ethics* 99 no. 2 (1989): 250–274.

Yuval-Davis, Nira, Georgie Wemyss, and Kathryn Cassidy. *Bordering.* John Wiley & Sons, 2019.

———. "Everyday Bordering, Belonging and the Reorientation of British Immigration Legislation." *Sociology* 52, no. 2 (2018): 228–44.

Zolberg, Aristide R. *A Nation by Design: Immigration Policy in the Fashioning of America.* Cambridge: Harvard University Press, 2009.

Zuckerman, Michael. *Peaceable Kingdoms: New England Towns in the Eighteenth Century.* New York: Alfred A. Knopf, 1970.

Index

Anthropology of Policy

Cris Shore and Susan Wright, editors

EDITORIAL BOARD

Laura Bear, Donald Brenneis, Janine Wedel, Dvora Yanow

Antinuclear Citizens: Sustainability Policy and
Grassroots Activism in Post-Fukushima Japan
Akihiro Ogawa
2023

The Alternative University: Lessons from Bolivarian Venezuela
Mariya P. Ivancheva
2023

Village Gone Viral: Hidden Dimensions of Traveling Policy Models
Marit Tolo Østebø
2021

Wild Policy: Indigeneity and the Unruly Logics of Intervention
Tess Lea
2020

The Gray Zone: Sovereignty, Human Smuggling, and
Undercover Police Investigation in Europe
Gregory Feldman
2019

Law Mart: Justice, Access, and For-Profit Law Schools
Riaz Tejani
2017

One Blue Child: Asthma, Responsibility, and the Politics of Global Health
Susanna Trnka
2017

The Orderly Entrepreneur: Youth, Education, and Governance in Rwanda
Catherine A. Honeyman
2016

Coercive Concern: Nationalism, Liberalism, and the Schooling of Muslim Youth
Reva Jaffe-Walter
2016

Fragile Elite: The Dilemmas of China's Top University Students
Susanne Bregnbæk
2016

Navigating Austerity: Currents of Debt along a South Asian River
Laura Bear
2015

Drugs, Thugs, and Diplomats: U.S. Policymaking in Colombia
Winifred Tate
2015

The authorized representative in the EU for product safety and compliance is:
Mare Nostrum Group B.V.
Mauritskade 21D
1091 GC Amsterdam
The Netherlands
Email address: gpsr@mare-nostrum.co.uk

KVK chamber of commerce number: 96249943

The authorized representative in the EU for product safety and compliance is:
Mare Nostrum Group
B.V Doelen 72
4831 GR Breda
The Netherlands

www.ingramcontent.com/pod-product-compliance
Lightning Source LLC
Chambersburg PA
CBHW030845270326
41928CB00007B/1224

9781503642393